I0167159

RAPIDLY REDUCE STRESS
WITH EMOTIONAL FREEDOM TECHNIQUE

Theodore W. Robinson

INNER HEALING PRESS

Rapidly Reduce Stress
with Emotional Freedom Technique

Copyright © 2012
Theodore W. Robinson

All rights reserved. No part of this
publication may be reproduced, stored in a
retrieval system, or transmitted in any form
or by any means, electronic, mechanical,
photocopying, recording, or otherwise,
without the prior written permission of the
copyright holder.

An Inner Healing Press Publication
www.innerhealingpress.com
www.centerforinnerhealing.com

TABLE OF CONTENTS

Rapid Reduction of Stress

Many people today suffer from stress of one sort of another. The problem is that when stress is left unresolved it can lead to a host of other problems over time. Stress is considered one of the biggest killers in the long run since it can lead to high blood pressure, heart disease, kidney failure and many, many more physical problems. The biggest areas of stress comes from relationships with others or struggling with too little time or money. Whatever it is that stresses you out, the fact of the matter is if stress is left unattended to, it will eventually kill you - or at least put you in a big hurt.

Many people turn to drugs and therapists to solve the problems for them, but the fact of the matter is the only reason most people are unhappy, upset and stressed out is because life didn't work out the way they had planned. That doesn't mean anyone is to blame. It is just a reflection of the human condition of believing the world should revolve around us and our desires rather than us working within the world around us.

So what's the answer? We know drugs only mask the problem and therapists are a great way of determining what our problems are, but they often don't have a real solution to offer other than an understanding ear. The answer lies within each of us. That's right, you hold the answer deep within yourself - it's only a matter of drawing it out and your stress can not only become more manageable, it can be resolved - so you can live in peace. So what is this so-called solution? We're going to tell you all about it in this book and teach you how to do it yourself.

We believe that the best approach to health and healing is to teach each person how they can help themselves. What we will teach you is Emotional Freedom Technique, or EFT, and it is intended to free you from all those negative thoughts, stress, self-limiting beliefs, pain and aberrant behaviors. It sounds too good to be true, doesn't it? It does work on all those things and much, much more. We'll be going through the entire process and then show you how to clear out all those old scars from negative experiences you're carrying around with you so you can start your life anew.

We'll first go through all the details of EFT with you to make sure you can do the technique correctly. Then we'll move on to the specifics of working with all kinds of stress and its resolution. After we're finished with that, we'll move on to the Personal Peace Procedure which is the ultimate personal process that leads to peace within you.

Emotional Freedom Technique

Emotional Freedom Technique (EFT) is a meridian based energy balancing system that is based upon a simple concept. The premise behind EFT is that a simple blockage in any energy meridian can result in a negative emotion, negative feeling, self-limiting belief, pain or aberrant behavior. All of that means stress of one sort or another. Those blockages are caused by physical, emotional or chemical traumas.

Once a blockage is in place, it will likely remain there until it is dislodged or dissipates with the passage of time. As long as the blockage is in place, the "Chi," which is a name for Universal Energy, will not be able to flow throughout your meridians and that is why negative feelings, beliefs and behaviors are caused. Once you eliminate the blockages, the energy can start to run again and then the negative feelings and emotions, self-limiting beliefs, pain and aberrant behavior are reduced or eliminated.

While many people in the West haven't yet heard about meridians, energy meridians have been used by Eastern physicians in Tibet and China for over 5,000 years. Eastern health care practitioners regularly "re-energize" the body by inserting needles at various strategic access points along the body's meridians (this is known as acupuncture), thereby reducing or eradicating all types of physical maladies. The needles somehow realign the energy within the meridians and returns the body back to normalcy.

Acupressure, is substantially the same as acupuncture, but without using needles. The pressure that is applied to the meridians can be done in many ways, but tapping with the tips of the fingers is the easiest and most effective. Emotional Freedom Technique is basically acupressure, coupled with focused attention on emotional issues. We also find that once emotional issues are resolved, then related physical issues often resolve, too.

We help our clients tap on the various meridian access points while they focus their attention on their predominant issue. We always use specific emotional issues to start. We simply have the client "tap" each of a series of "meridian access points" located on the surface of the skin 5-7 times at each point with two fingers of their dominant hand (if you're right handed, then that is your dominant hand. If left handed, then use your left.) The access points are generally located at the starting point of each meridian and meridians run the entire length of the body with a primary access point at each end. There is nothing unusual about the appearance of the skin at those points, so you will have to learn where they are located by referring to the diagram at the back of the book. However, once you learn the points, they are easy to remember.

By tapping on the points repeatedly, you effectively break or dislodge any blockages that may exist within the meridians. That, in turn, reduces or eliminates the negative emotions and stress you were feeling. It's similar to tapping the top of a straw that has a little bit of milk left in the middle of it. As you tap the top of the straw, you break the vacuum above where the milk is located and the milk dissipates easily. Once the blockage is broken, air can flow through the straw again just as the Chi (life force energy) flows through your meridians once any blockages are dislodged. Once the blockage is gone you naturally go back to feeling good again - your normal state of being.

As mentioned earlier, blockages are formed when you suffer some sort of trauma, either physical, emotional or chemical in nature. Trauma doesn't have to mean that you get hit by a truck (although that certainly would be traumatic). It can be any trauma, large or small, that has a negative impact upon you and your meridian system. As long as your body/mind interpreted the impact as a trauma of any nature, a blockage will likely result, and as long as the blockage remains, you will continue to suffer from negative thoughts, negative emotions, stress, self- limiting beliefs, pain and aberrant behavior.

It is important to know there is no diagnosis or specific treatment used when doing EFT because EFT practitioners are not generally licensed health care practitioners. Instead, we usually act as coaches to assist our clients to focus on their specific issues and help them describe it in detail as they tap on all the meridian access points we use in EFT. By tapping all the meridian access points, you can't miss the ones that are blocked. Also, by tapping all the meridian access points every time we do the technique, there is no diagnosis or specific treatment needed to address the particular issue. That assures that we can't miss the blocked meridians that are causing the negative emotions or self-limiting beliefs.

When it comes to stress reduction, EFT is superb at resolving it quickly and effectively because it works on the person who is feeling stressed out by outside influences, instead of trying to change the other person or circumstance that is stressing that person out. As a result, you become self-empowered to resolve your stresses from within rather than trying to change everyone and everything around you.

We recognize that all healing is an "inside job," meaning each of us actually causes our own stress when we expect the world to be "our way" rather than the way it is. People tend to perceive the world through the filters of their minds which are skewed by their past experiences in life.

We call that the "writing on our walls" meaning the "Rules" we've written on the inside of our brains on how to deal with the world. For instance, if things have been difficult in your life so far, then it is likely you will view the world as a dangerous and unforgiving place and deal with it defensively, keeping your distance from others and dealing with everyone as if they're going to harm you or take advantage of you. That can be very stressful.

On the other hand, if you've had good experiences in your life, you may see the world in the opposite way and feel like others can be trusted and accepted. That usually leads to feelings of trust, compassion and peace. It all depends upon your upbringing and your early life experiences as to how you are likely to respond to the world now and how much stress you will feel in any given situation.

When we first began "writing on our walls" (meaning establishing our belief system), it usually reflected the judgments and beliefs we formed early in our lives about everything with which we came into contact. You may have liked ice cream and hated spinach or something along those lines. You form preconceived notions about almost everything with which you later come into contact with because of the original "writing on your walls." Many times, those beliefs are self-limiting which means they quietly hold us back before we even get started in many things. It's like the operating software that often comes with a computer when you buy it. If there is no pre-existing command in the software to do what you want it to do - the computer doesn't know what to do with new information. The same holds true if a computer is programmed with a program that says it is not to accept some types of information (such as a security system that's programmed to not accept spam or junk email). It sometimes gets confused when something comes into your computer that is really an acceptable email, and because of its programming, the computer sends it to the trash. The "writing on its walls" kept it from giving it a new look, just as our prior programming stops us from being open to new ideas too.

Similarly, our "writing" often comes from our earliest life experiences and how we related to them or judged them. That means that when we were children, we were either imbued with certain beliefs about the world and ourselves by our parents and teachers that subsequently affected everything we did throughout our life - or we had experiences that affected us the rest of our life in much the same way. The "writings" that result from those early experiences can be as simple as "I'm a bad boy" or "I'm a good girl," to things as complex as "I never get any attention by being good, so at least I'll get some attention by being bad" or "nothing I ever do is ever good enough - so why bother?" Those are self-limiting beliefs which have gone wrong. In other situations, you may have the thought that "I can't do it" or "I'm not smart enough" or "I'm not pretty enough," etc. and those beliefs then tend to hold you back from even trying.

In fact, that can take place in many ways throughout your life if you succumb to those self-limiting beliefs. When you think you're "not smart enough" it will often hold you back from seeking admission to college or from applying for a better job. When you think you're not pretty enough, you may find that you settle for the first guy that shows you any interest for fear there won't be another who will come along. That

5

type of thinking can change your life forever - all based upon your earliest childhood experiences. Can you imagine if you can change that type of thinking? Keep reading - you can.

There are many, many "writings" on the inside of the walls of our minds and most of them affect us for better or worse depending upon our earliest judgments in life. Worst of all, many unreasonable or immature judgments made during our childhood stay with us long into adulthood and often hold us back from meeting our true potential. At least that's the way it's been up until now. Now you can use EFT to address and resolve those negative writings, and eliminate those which haven't served you well to this point in your life. Once you eliminate the negative or self-limiting beliefs, you can then insert new ideas and positive programming in their place. Then you can allow yourself to focus on the remaining "good" or positive writings on your walls and evolve yourself into a more peaceful person. In fact, life can become peaceful, effortless and fun again.

Remember, those negative feelings aren't just in your mind. They are actually the result of physical blockages within your energy meridian system. From the perspective of Emotional Freedom Technique, every negative emotion is the result of a blockage in your energy meridians due to a traumatic event in your life. That blockage and subsequent self-limiting thoughts, negative beliefs or negative feelings will usually last throughout the rest of your life unless the blockage is broken. For example, have you ever known someone who is still afraid of frogs, spiders or small animals because they were initially frightened by their older siblings or friends as they lay in their bed asleep? Those people still have some fear that they'll find another frog in their bed at night and that fear is just as real now as it was for them when they were traumatized as a child. Yet, it's actually nothing more than a simple blockage in their meridian system that can be eliminated by tapping on one of the meridian access points. That's the amazing quality of EFT, it works quickly and effectively and it's permanent.

When it comes to stress, the same technique is used and the same relief is available to you. The difference with stressful situations is determining how the original meridian blockage occurred and why. Most of the time stress is caused by the judgment of your ego simply being different than the judgment of other people's egos.

No matter how the stress in your life occurs, if it is allowed to remain unresolved, it will eventually fester inside you and eventually cause physical problems for you. That's why we wrote this book, so you won't have to remain stressed any longer. We're going to explain and demonstrate everything you need to know to rapidly reduce your stress using EFT.

Of course, the question arises, what does EFT have to do with stress? Well, EFT is just an effective technique that can literally do away with stress in short order. The best part is it is very self-empowering because it puts you in control of your stress once you learn the technique. Then the question arises: Which energy meridian do I tap on to eliminate my stress? Again, the answer is easy. Tap them all. That way, you don't have to diagnose the precise problem or try to figure out how to deal with any specific type of stress by tapping just the "correct" meridians. Instead, we always tap on every meridian every time so we can't miss the one that's blocked. In fact, by tapping them all, you're always assured of success - as long as your mind is focused on the right issue and you're feeling the stress as completely as possible.

The first thing you need to do is identify the stressful issue that is bothering you the most at this time. It's always best to focus your attention on a very specific and emotional issue, rather than a generalized one. That way, you can focus your attention like a laser beam which will usually give you better results.

Once you've identified your specific issue, you want to give it a title (something like a movie title - just a few descriptive words) and then you'll want to establish a SUDS for it. A **SUDS**, (used in all hospital Emergency Rooms), is an acronym for **S**ubjective **U**nit of **D**iscomfort **S**cale. We use it to first establish how badly you feel about the stressful issue and then to monitor how much that stress dissipates as we use EFT to reduce it.

Remember, you always use a scale of 1-10 with 10 being the most uncomfortable (characterized by crying, extreme upset, etc.) down to 0 which means you can no longer feel it or access the feelings surrounding the issue at all. We use this type of subjective scale because everyone's pain or discomfort threshold is unique to them and we just ask the client how they're feeling and ask them to put a number to it to the best of their ability. The best way to do this is just say the first number that comes to mind based upon how you feel at the time. You will then use EFT to work through each issue until your SUDS on each one is down to zero.

Please note that Emotional Freedom Technique is unique in that the Set-Up and Sequence (tapping) procedures use some of the <u>most negative</u> wordings possible in order to achieve its goals. That's because in our experience, by getting you to say very negative words, you are more likely to feel your negative feelings to the fullest extent. By doing that and then tapping all the meridian access points at the same time, you will be better able to heal the underlying issue quickly and completely.

We recognize that many people recoil from using any negative wording. They often worry that if they say anything negative to their subconscious mind, "it might latch onto it" and they will be negatively affected by it. However, with EFT, **the exact opposite is true** . . . **as long as you're tapping at the same time**. In fact, we usually use **the most** negative wording available because we've discovered that by saying the most negative statements possible, **while doing the tapping procedure**, the deepest negative feelings arise for most people because the very negative words puts them in touch with their most negative feelings. That then causes <u>larger</u> blockages within their meridians (which is what we <u>want</u> to do). By doing that, it allows us to <u>unblock</u> the meridians more with the tapping than if the meridians were only partially blocked. In other words, the more you feel the pain, the more you can heal it. In this way we can rapidly remove the stress, negative emotions and self-limiting beliefs in your mind and return you to peace more quickly.

We've also discovered that when we don't use the most negative wording possible, our clients are often left with some residue of the old negative emotions and they don't get as much relief as they do when we use the most negative wording. Remember, the more you feel it, the more you heal it with EFT.

How to Use the Technique

Once you identify the specific issue you want to work on, determine your SUDS level between 1-10 and you're ready to start. If you can't or don't feel comfortable using such a scale, then you may assume you're starting at a 10 on the SUDS scale and you keep tapping until you can't feel or access the issue any longer (that means you're at a 0). Many people start out with a 10 and end up with a zero after just a few rounds of tapping at which point they can't even access the issue at all.

Once you've established your SUDS, the process starts with the "**Set-Up**" which we will go over below. This is a procedure where you continuously tap with the first two fingers on your dominant hand, on the Karate Chop spot, which is the side of your non-dominant palm/hand while you state the problem and end your statement with words like, "*Yet I love and accept myself nonetheless.*"

By doing this, you are effectively "talking" to the subconscious mind which is the part of the mind that is often programmed to feel negatively about things (that's the writing on the walls we mentioned). We view this as a "normalization" process between the conscious and subconscious levels of the mind. By doing this, you start the healing process in an accepting fashion, telling the subconscious (which is like a 3 year old emotionally) that regardless of what it may have "done wrong" (in your conscious mind's judgment), it is loved and accepted nonetheless. For those who can't or won't say they "love and accept themselves", they can simply say they are "doing the best I can" or "I accept myself" or "I'm okay."

The initial Set-Up process also automatically corrects for any "psychological reversal" that might be present in your body. By simply tapping on the side of your palm on the Karate Chop (KC) spot (see diagram) as you say the Set-Up words, any reversal is eliminated and it insures that the rest of the tapping procedure will work just fine. That is why you tap the side of the hand at both the beginning and end of the process.

The "**Sequence**," is the actual tapping on the meridian access points that removes the blockages within the rest of the meridians. The

Sequence immediately follows the Set-Up and consists of tapping each of the meridian access points 5-7 times while you say some reminder phrases (reminder phrases are parts of the phrases used in the Set-Up) to keep your mind focused upon the issue. We start with the eyebrow point and move on from point to point until you end with the top of the head point. At each meridian access point, you say a Reminder Phrase to keep your mind focused on the specific issue. You may change the words as you go from point to point or you may say the same words as you move along like "this stress."

This process will generally reduce your emotional discomfort level progressively until your SUDS is down to 0. Once the issue is accessed as you tap and your SUDS starts to move downward, it is only a matter of time before it's completely resolved. On occasion, another similar issue or a related issue will pop up so soon that it will often fool you into thinking that the original issue never resolved, but if you carefully feel the original feeling, you'll likely notice it is a different aspect of the first feeling - with a twist.

Different Aspects

When a different aspect of the original issue arises, it usually doesn't announce itself in advance. Instead, it just pops up seemingly out of nowhere and presents itself. An aspect is usually closely related to the original issue or is part of it, just a little different. If the new feeling arises while you're already tapping on a particular issue, it may be missed or you may think your original issue worsened. When that happens, your SUDS goes up instead of down.

Whenever the intensity of the issue you're working on increases it is usually one of two things: either you are finally feeling the issue fully because you're talking about it as you tap or you have accessed a different aspect of the original issue that is stronger than the original issue. Both will increase your SUDS unexpectedly. When that happens, don't panic. Just feel into the new issue or different aspect of the original issue and address it with appropriate words that include any new feelings about it.

Here is an example:

The original issue is "*I have so much stress at my job I just can't stand it any longer.*" After you have done the Set-Up and a Sequence once or twice, it may strike you that it is not your job that is stressing you out, but your boss or a co-worker. Instead of continuing to tap on the more general issue of the job, you may change your wording to include that specific person. That way, you get more accurate about the real issue at hand and that way you'll get much better results more rapidly.

The normal EFT process consists of a series of Set-Ups and Sequences in which you repeat slightly different reminder phrases to address the issue from different perspectives. You use the Sequence repeatedly on the original issue (using the reduction in the SUDS level as a guide), until that issue is reduced down to zero. Each time you finish a round, there will usually be a reduction in your SUDS number which you should acknowledge in your next Set-Up phrase by saying

"*Even though there has been a decrease in how much stress I feel, I still have some stress to eliminate and I love and accept myself nonetheless.*"

Continue with a Sequence after that and change the wording of each subsequent Sequence to match any reductions in your SUDS until the issue is down to 0. Again, the best way to tell if you're at a zero is when you can't focus on or even access the issue any longer. This is sometimes surprising to people because they suddenly cannot even think about what they were feeling when they started and they never had such an experience before - but it happens quite normally.

Once that happens, the next issue will automatically rise to the surface of your awareness and make itself known to you. You then start the entire process all over again with the new issue. We often explain this by likening it to a pile of plates stacked in a spring-loaded plate dispenser in a cafeteria. You use EFT on the initial plate and as you finish it, the next one automatically comes up on its own and then you start the process all over again with the new "plate."

When a new aspect arises, the succeeding rounds (issues) may be related to the first issue, but usually have a different twist or aspect to them from the first issue that arose. This is normal. Just keep working on each "plate" as it arises within your consciousness and soon, you'll feel much less stressed.

The Apex Effect

Some people are so surprised by the fact that an issue can be reduced so quickly using EFT that they don't believe it and their mind often rejects it because it appears to be "too good and too quick to be true." This is called the Apex Effect. Effectively what we consider the "higher" part of the mind, the conscious mind, rejects what is actually under the control of the subconscious mind and the energy system of the body. It decides that since it didn't take a long time to get over a very serious emotional or physical issue, then it can't be real. The conscious mind will then try to rationalize or attribute such quick results to "those vitamins I took three days ago finally kicked in," or "that chiropractic adjustment from last week finally made my pain go away," disregarding the fact that the vitamins or the adjustment had nothing to do with it or it would have happened sooner. The best thing to remember is, if you just used EFT on a particular issue and you can no longer access it or feel it, you found relief because of using EFT.

Full Sequence vs. Short Cut

The way EFT was first taught, the **Full Sequence** consisted of tapping all the points on the head, face, collarbone and underarm as well as tapping all the finger points at the corners of the nails and the Nine Gamut. The **Short Cut** uses everything but the finger points and the Nine Gamut process. From our experience, it is just as effective as the Full Sequence and it saves time. For the purpose of this book, all we will be using is the Short Cut because it is fast and effective.

The rest of the Sequence consists of tapping each of the fingernails at the point where the nail bed turns upward towards the end of the nail closest to the thumb 5-7 times each. It also includes the entire Nine Gamut procedure which includes a neuro-linguistic programming regimen. It's up to you whether you include them in your use of the technique or not. We generally use only the shortcut and use these other processes when the shortcut alone isn't working as quickly as we had hoped. Visit our web site for more information about these two parts of the process.

Turbo-Charging the Sequence

To make the entire process even more effective, you can use both hands to tap both sides of each access point at the same time. That means you would tap both "above the eye" points simultaneously, both the "side of eye" points simultaneously and so on. The meridians are bilateral in nature (meaning they run on both sides of the center of the body) and they act like a liquid leveling device (in other words, a long clear hose with colored water in it that seeks its own level on both ends of the hose over long distances - this is used by masons to level foundations). In this way, both sides of meridians strive to remain balanced or at an equal level on each side of the center of the body.

When one side of the two meridians becomes blocked (due to trauma), the other side then changes its relative energetic position in order to counterbalance the blockage in the blocked meridian. When you tap on the blocked side and dislodge the blockage, the energy in that meridian becomes free to flow again. At that point, the energy in the other side of the two meridians starts to flow again and they will both continue to flow until they are balanced with each other again. This can take a little time and that's why it sometimes takes a little extra time for the issue to clear once you've completed the tapping sequence. It also explains why we accept a SUDS of 1 or 2 rather than demanding a zero every time before we stop. Even a 1or 2 will usually become a zero with the passage of time.

The Eye Ladder

If you get the SUDS number down to a 3 or under, this is a simple process that will eliminate the remaining negative charge. It's called the Eye Ladder.

To do the Eye Ladder, tap continuously with two fingers on the back of the opposite hand between the ring finger bone (metacarpal) and the pinky bone, in the "valley" part of the hand, on the Nine Gamut point (point 14 on the diagram). As you continue to tap, focus your eyes (without moving your head back) upward as high as possible. Then, as if you were coming down a ladder with your eyes, move your eyes downward in five equal steps until your eyes are looking downward as far as possible. You can also do the technique by moving your eyes from the bottom up five times. Each time you move your eyes, repeat your reminder phrase such as "this stress," "anger," "this remaining anger," or "all remaining anger." Continue this process until you are at a zero. That usually only takes only one Eye Ladder.

The Nine Gamut

The Nine Gamut is actually a synthesis of neuro-linguistic programming and eye movements in addition to continuous tapping on the back of the hand on the Nine Gamut point. This balances the two sides of the mind, the conscious and the subconscious, and is a powerful adjunct to the primary Sequence when a negative issue won't budge using only the Short Cut.

To do the Nine Gamut technique, continuously tap on the back of the hand in the valley between the pinky and ring fingers bones on the hand (point 14, Nine Gamut point), while doing the movements directed below.

Without moving the head:
- Look straight forward for 5 taps on the back of the hand with your eyes open
- Close your eyes for 5 taps
- Look down and hard to the right for 5 taps
- Look down and hard to the left for 5 taps
- Move your eyes in a clockwise circle starting at 12 o'clock and return to 12 o'clock
- Reverse the movement starting at 12 o'clock and return to 12 o'clock (be sure movement is smooth)
- Count 1, 2, 3, 4, 5

14

- Sing a tune (Happy Birthday works well)
- Count 1, 2, 3, 4, 5

While doing the circular movement, it is helpful to have someone else move their fingers or hand in a clockwise and counterclockwise fashion for you so that your eyes can follow them. It gives you something to focus on while moving them. Ask them to watch your eyes closely as you follow their hand. If the other person notices that your eyes are "jumping" or "skipping" parts of the circle, have them move their fingers back and forth across that section of the circle where they jumped while they remind you to concentrate on following their fingers. It has been our experience that when the eyes can follow the circular movement smoothly, the issue being worked on often vanishes completely almost immediately.

As for why we count, this is a rote memorization process which utilizes the left side of the brain and the singing uses the right side or subconscious mind. Alternating the two sides of the brain helps to re-balance them and helps them work together.

The EFT Process

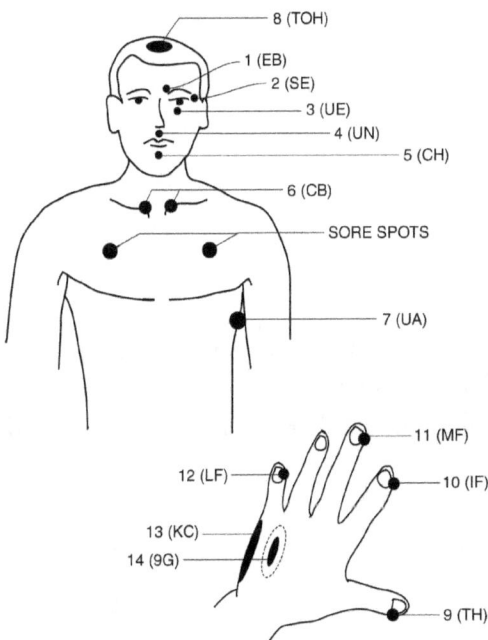

It's now time to get started with the EFT process. We start every EFT session, whether in a private session or a group, with a round of "Resistance to Change." We do this because it is normal to resist changing your existing belief system or programming. When we address that resistance at the very outset, you will have a much easier time accomplishing change to occur on your issues.

We have included the diagram on the left to assist you.

Resistance to Change, the Set-Up and Sequence

The Set-Up:

The Set-Up is when we start focusing the mind on the issue you want to resolve. As we start the Set-Up process, we remove any psychological reversal that could stand in the way of relieving your stress as we simultaneously focus the mind with words. We do this by tapping continuously with the first two fingers of your dominant hand on the Karate Chop spot, which is located on the opposing hand, on the side of the palm. At the same time, we say a sentence to focus the mind on the issue. It sounds like this:

"Even though I may have some resistance to change, I love and accept myself."

By doing this, we first state how stressed out we are about our problem and then finish up with "I love and accept myself." This starts the healing process by having the judgmental conscious mind (which is stressed out about the job), tell the innocent subconscious mind it loves and accepts it regardless of whether the problem with the job is its fault or not. We generally repeat this phrase 3 times before we start the Sequence. The second two phrases may stay exactly the same as the first or they may vary somewhat as follows:

"Even though I know I must have some resistance to change because I'm not changing those things I want to change in my life, I love and accept myself nonetheless."

"Even though I have a ton of resistance to change, I'm doing the best I can about it and I love and accept myself completely."

Once we are done with the Set-Up we move on to the Sequence which means we start tapping each meridian point 5-7 times while saying Reminder Phrases at each access point which relate back to the words used in the Set-Up.

The Sequence:

The simplest way to do the Sequence is to just say one reminder phrase at all meridian access points. For instance, the simplest phrase is just: *"This resistance to change."* That reminds the subconscious mind what we're working on as we tap all the meridians.

While this simple system works, it has been our experience that when an issue is complex or not being fully felt at the time of the tapping, then a little more complex method works better. With the more complex style, we use a stream of consciousness to say whatever the feeling is about the issue that we're feeling within. However, not everyone is adept at this style of using words, so it may take some time to practice getting in touch with the feelings and using the appropriate words.

There are a number of examples in this book on how to access stressful issues more effectively so you can reduce that stress more rapidly. Of course, it is always up to you as to which approach feels best to you, but we also suggest you change the words in the examples to fit exactly how you feel as you go through the Sequences after you've used the suggested words the first time through.

The Sequence consists of tapping 5-7 times on each meridian access point while saying reminder phrases to keep the mind focused on the issue at hand. The wording would sound like this as we continue with the issue we started above.

EB (eyebrow) - "I must have some resistance to change."
SE (side of eye) - "I know that because I'm not changing much."
UE (under eye) - "I can't seem to let go of my past."
UN (under nose) - "I want to let go of this resistance to change."
CB (collarbone) - "I have a ton of resistance to change."
UA (under arm) - "Nothing is changing in my life because of it."
TH (top of head) - "I let go of all remaining resistance to change."
KC (karate chop) - "All this resistance to change leaves me now."

That constitutes one full Sequence that contains various alternative statements about resistance to change and how it adversely affects you. The words can be changed as much as you feel is necessary to address this issue. You can also simply say words to the effect of "This resistance to change" and repeat them on each access point exactly the same, rather than changing them all the time. That often makes it easier for those who are just starting to use EFT. The technique will still work.

Once you've finished the first Sequence, take a deep breath and check into how you feel about the issue now to see if your SUDS has changed at all. Regardless of whether it changed or not, always make a remark within the next Set-Up about how you feel now and then go back to your Reminder phrases again with each point. That way it honors what has happened (or not) within your meridians. It would sound like this - as part of the second Set-Up and Sequence round.

2nd Set-Up:
Tap continuously on the Karate Chop point as you say the words:
"Even though I'm feeling a little bit less resistant to change, I'm still feeling it and know that I'm not willing to change easily. Yet, I love and accept myself nonetheless."

2nd Sequence:
Tap 5-7 times on each point as you say the words:
EB (eyebrow) - "I'm feeling a little bit less resistant to change."
SE (side of eye) - "I still don't want to change much."
UE (under eye) - "I don't like change much."
UN (under nose) - "I still am not looking forward to change."
CB (collarbone) - "I feel stressed out about change."
UA (under arm) - "I still don't like to change."
TH (top of head) - "I let go of all remaining resistance to change."
KC (karate chop) - "I'm feeling a lot less resistant to change now."

3rd Sequence:
EB (eyebrow) - "I'm starting to realize I don't have to remain resistant."
SE (side of eye) - "I still would rather not have to change."
UE (under eye) - "But my resistance is reducing now."
UN (under nose) - "I'm starting to see that change can be a good thing."
CB (collarbone) - "The only constant in life is change."
UA (under arm) - "I feel I can now start to embrace change in my life."
TH (top of head) - "I let go of any resistance to change left within me."
KC (karate chop) - "I'm feeling a lot better about changing now."
KC (karate chop) - "I know this is going to work for me."

That's how 3 Sequences can be put together in succession and work effectively to eliminate resistance to change and how we add a "re-frame" on the end of them. By **re-framing** the overall issue from a very negative feeling to a positive one, the entire issue of resistance to change can change dramatically from very negative to positive in the space of 10 minutes.

Once you realize how effective this technique can be for you, it is then time to work on your stressful issues. To do this, you need only take an inventory of whatever stresses you the most, set a SUDS and start tapping. It's as simple as that. Remember, whenever you use EFT, you want to make sure you feel the stress or whatever other negative emotion you're feeling as fully as possible. Otherwise, you will miss some of it and leave it within your meridian to grow into a full-fledged problem again. So always make sure to do your best to use words that bring up the negative emotion the best.

EFT Summary

The Basic Recipe - Set a Level of Discomfort from 0-10 Before Starting

1. The Setup . . . Repeat the statement 3 times:
While continuously tapping either the Karate Chop point on either hand (for specific issues) or rubbing one of the two Sore Spots (for intense and/or generalized issues), say "Even though I have this anger, frustration, fear, etc., I deeply and completely accept myself."

2. The Sequence . . . Tap about 5-7 times with two fingers of your dominant on each of the following energy points found on the attached diagram while repeating the Reminder Phrase at each point.

1	2	3	4	5	6	7	8	9	10	11	12	13
EB	SE	UE	UN	CH	CB	UA	TOH	TH	IF	MF	LF	KC

3. The 9 Gamut Procedure . . .Continuously tap on the Gamut point (9G) (14) while performing each of these 9 actions (The 9 Gamut is not ordinarily used unless necessary):

(1) Eyes open (2) Eyes closed (3) Eyes hard down right (4) Eyes hard down left (5) Roll eyes in full circle clockwise (6) Roll eyes in circle in other direction (7) Count to 5 (8) Hum 2 seconds of a song (9) Count to 5. (Re-evaluate your discomfort level before continuing)

4. The 2nd Sequence... Tap between 5-7 times using 2 fingers on each of the energy points while repeating the Reminder Phrase at each point.

Note: In subsequent rounds The Setup affirmation and the Reminder Phrase are adjusted to reflect that you are addressing "this remaining"... (problem) etc. (continue until at a zero).

<u>Legend</u>:

1 - Eye Brow	5 - Chin	9 - Thumb
2 - Side of Eye	6 - Collar Bone	10 - Index Finger
3 - Under Eye	7 - Under Arm	11 - Middle
4 - Under Nose	8 - Top of Head	Finger
		12 - Little Finger
		13 - Karate Chop

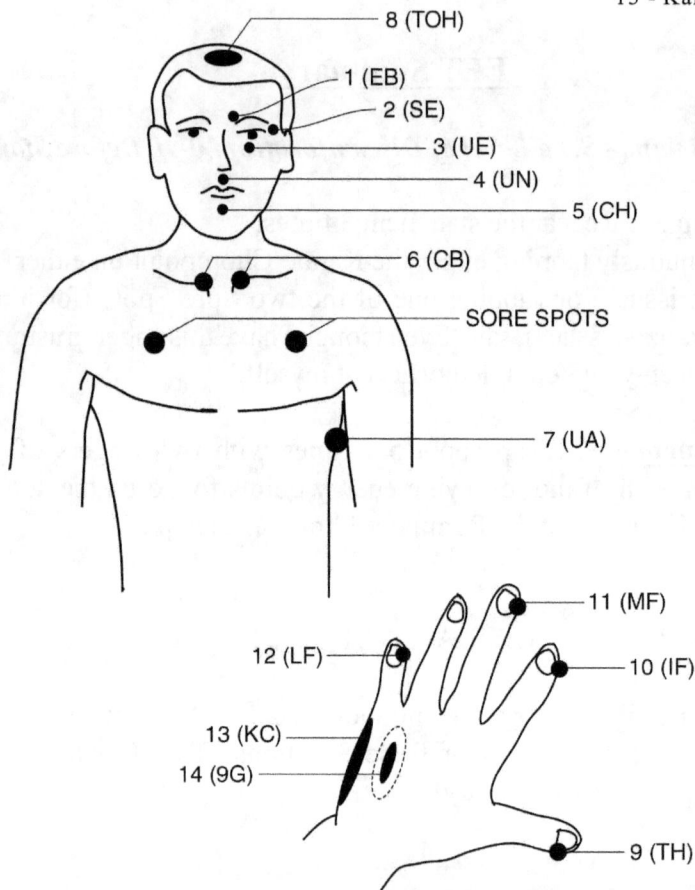

8 (TOH)
1 (EB)
2 (SE)
3 (UE)
4 (UN)
5 (CH)
6 (CB)
SORE SPOTS
7 (UA)
11 (MF)
12 (LF)
10 (IF)
13 (KC)
14 (9G)
9 (TH)

Specific Stressful Issues

Now that you know how to do EFT and have taken care of releasing your resistance to change, it's time to start working on specific stressful issues. We will provide you with specific wording for each issue so you can work on them yourself. Of course, if the words provided don't exactly address your issue, feel free to modify the Set-Up and/or Sequence to include the words that will apply to your specific issue best.

Remember, as you do EFT, the way to get the very best results is to feel the emotions attached to the issue as fully as possible. It has been our experience that the more you feel the negativity of your issue, the better the ultimate results will be for you.

My Spouse/Partner Doesn't Understand Me

First determine your SUDS (Subjective Unit of Discomfort Scale between 1-10 with 10 being the worst feeling about the issue.)

Set-Up:
"Even though my Spouse/Partner doesn't understand me, I love and accept myself fully and completely."

"Even though s/he always wants everything his/her own way and it frustrates me and stresses me out, I love and accept myself anyway."

"I can't believe s/he refuses to see things my way. What's wrong with him/her? Whenever I want to do something, they never agree - and I'm tired of it!"

Sequence:
EB -"My Spouse/Partner doesn't understand me."
SE -"I can't stand it when s/he doesn't get it!"
UE -"Why am I always the one who has to give in? I don't want to give in any more."
UN -"This sucks! I can't stand him/her!"
UM -"I'm afraid if I say anything, our entire relationship will end."
CB -"I want to compromise, but I don't want to be taken advantage of."
UA -"I want to let this go, but I can't - yet."

TH -*"I really love my Spouse/Partner, but sometimes s/he just annoys the hell out of me."*

KC - *"I've been so stressed out about us, but it's feeling better already and I know it's going to be resolved."*

Stop, take a deep breath, and check your SUDS to see if anything has changed yet. Take note of any change and immediately start another round with a new Set-Up and Sequence.

2nd Set-Up:

"Even though I'm feeling (<u>a little bit better</u> - or however you're feeling about it) about this stress between my Spouse/Partner, I still have a lot of stress to work out about us, and I love and accept myself no matter how this works out."

2nd Sequence:

EB -*"I'm feeling a little better about this stress between me and my Spouse/Partner, but they still don't seem to understand me."*

SE -*"I know we just misunderstand each other, but it is still upsetting."*

UE -*"Why does s/he think I always have to be the one to give in? I'm tired of it!."*

UN -*"I love him/her, but I sometimes wonder whether they love me."*

UM -*"I know they love me, but sometimes they don't act like it."*

CB -*"I want to work this out and I guess as long as I'm heard I can do it."*

UA -*"I want to let this go now."*

TH -*"I love my Spouse/Partner and know we can work this out between us - when we remember we love one another."*

KC - *"I do love my Spouse/Partner and this is going to end now."*

Stop, take a deep breath, and check your SUDS to see if anything has changed yet. Take note of any change and immediately start another round with a new Set-Up and Sequence.

3rd Set-Up:

"I'm feeling (<u>much better</u> - or however you're feeling about it) about this stress and I know it's going to be completely resolved and we'll get along just fine from now on, and I love and accept myself fully and completely."

3rd Sequence:

EB - "I'm feeling a lot better about this stress and I realize it was just a disagreement between me and my Spouse/Partner."

SE - "Whether they understand me or not, I understand myself better and I'm now more willing to deal with our differences."

UE - "I don't have to always win. It's not a matter of winning anyway."

UN - "I always love him/her, regardless of how s/he acts towards me."

UM - "I know we just think differently sometimes and when we remember that we love each other, these conflicts dissolve more easily."

CB - "I am working this out within me already and I like that."

UA - "I let this conflict go now."

TH - "I love and embrace my Spouse/Partner and know we love each other no matter what goes on between us at times."

KC - "I love my Spouse/Partner and this stress is ended now."

Stop, take a deep breath, and check your SUDS to see if there is any residue of the stressful feelings left. If there is, go back to any round above and do it again and again until the feeling is gone. Change any wording you feel does not apply to you to make it apply to you.

Employment Issues

Many people have various issues regarding their jobs. Some have issues about trying to find a job. You may use these examples to tap on the issues offered and change the wording as you require to address your specific issue.

I Can't Find a Job

First set your SUDS on your issue revolving around being unemployed and not being able to find a job, then start with the Set-Up as follows:

Set-Up:

"Even though I'm a capable worker, I've been laid off and can't find a job and it's really frustrating and upsetting. I want to work and

23

nobody wants to hire me. Yet, I'm doing the best that I can no matter what happens."

    "Even though I'm competent at everything I do, how do I demonstrate that to an interviewer when they never give me a chance? I'm so frustrated, angry and stressed out I don't know what to do with myself, but I'm doing the best I can to deal with this situation."

Sequence:
EB - "I can't find a job and it's really frustrating!"
SE - "I can't stand it when an interviewer isn't listening!"
UE - "What am I supposed to do? How am I supposed to act to get a job?"
UN - "I feel like giving up!"
UM - "I'm afraid to go on interviews any longer. They all seem so worthless and a waste of time."
CB - "I want to do well in my next interview, but I'm now becoming worried that I'll never find a job."
UA - "I want to act normally, but I'm so nervous, I rarely act normal any more."
TH - "I feel like this is all a waste of time. I'm afraid nobody will every employ me again and I don't know what to do."
KC - "I've been so stressed out about being unemployed, it seems the interviewer can "smell" the fear in me as soon as I walk in the door."

    Stop, take a deep breath, and check your SUDS to see if anything has changed yet. Take note of any change and immediately start another round with a new Set-Up and Sequence.

2ⁿᵈ Set-Up:
    "Even though I'm feeling (<u>a little bit better</u> - or however you're feeling about it) about not being able to find work, I still have a lot of worry and stress to cope with before my next interview. I sure hope this works because I sure need a job, and I love and accept myself no matter how this all works out."

2ⁿᵈ Sequence:

EB - "I'm feeling a little better about this stress I've been in about getting a job, but I'm still worried it won't really go away completely."

SE - "I know I have to calm down to do well in an interview, but it's very upsetting and intimidating to go into an interview for me."

UE - "Why does it seem like I can't calm down when I know that I'm excellent at what they want me to do in this next job?"

UN - "I actually believe I am a little calmer already and I like that. I think this is going to work for me."

UM - "I know this can work for me, but I still have a little nagging fear about it."

CB - "I really want to work this out so I can go into the next interview and do well."

UA - "I now choose to let this fear go completely."

TH - "I now realize I've been making too much of this whole thing and I can make a different choice about how I feel and change how I come across in the next interview."

KC - "I know this is going to work out and that I'll do well at finding a job."

Stop, take a deep breath, and check your SUDS to see if anything has changed yet. Take note of any change and immediately start another round with a new Set-Up and Sequence.

3rd Set-Up:

"I'm feeling (much better - or however you're feeling about it) about this stress about being unemployed and trying to find a job. I now realize I've been too stressed out to find a job and I now realize I can calm myself down and find a job much easier and I love and accept myself fully and completely no matter how the next interview turns out."

3rd Sequence:

EB - "I'm feeling a lot better about this situation I'm in and know that things are going to work out now."

SE - "No matter how the next interview turns out, I've already changed my mind and am a lot less stressed than I was when I started."

UE - "I don't have to worry so much any more. I am a capable and competent person and I would be an asset for them if they hire me."

25

UN -"There are no 'if's' about it. They will hire me and it will be a win/win situation all around."

UM -"I know this is already working because I'm already feeling more confident and I know things are going to improve from now on."

CB -"I have made a choice to be more self-confident and release any remaining worry and fear and embrace confidence instead."

UA -"I accept myself completely, knowing I have much to offer."

TH -"I choose to be confident and self-assured in every interview and exude a positive attitude at all times."

KC - "I like this and I know this is going to work."

Stop, take a deep breath, and check your SUDS to see if there is any residue of the stressful feelings left. If there is, go back to any round above and do it again and again until the feeling is gone. Change any wording you feel does not apply to you to make it apply to you.

Money Issues

Many people suffer from money issues. Many don't feel like they have enough money, while others are perverted by having too much money. While money is really only a medium of exchange or power, many people mistake it for other things such as happiness and satisfaction and then later suffer the results of those mistakes. We will endeavor to go through a couple of different money issues and you may change the words as you require to make the Set-Ups fit your situation.

I Never Have Enough Money

First set your SUDS on your issue revolving around being unemployed and then start with the Set-Up as follows:

Set-Up:
"Even though it often feel like I never have enough money, I love and accept myself nonetheless."

"Even though I always do the best I can, money seems to elude me most of the time and then I get so stressed out thinking about money and

how much I want to have more money coming in to me and my family. I'm very frustrated, nervous and stressed out about the whole thing and can't sleep at night as a result, but I'm doing the best I can to deal with the entire situation."

"Even though I just never seem to have enough money to pay all my bills or give my family whatever they need, I love and accept myself nonetheless."

Sequence:
EB - "I never feel like I have enough money and I'm always worried!"
SE - "I can't believe this is happening to me!"
UE - "What am I supposed to do? How can I earn more money when nobody wants to give me a job?"
UN - "I feel like this will never get any better."
UM - "I'm afraid I'm going to ruin my family and we're all going to starve."
CB - "I want to do better, but nobody wants to help me."
UA - "I want to make more money, but I'm totally lost at this point."
TH - "I feel like I'm wasting my time. I'm afraid nobody will ever give me a decent job and I don't know what to do."
KC - "I've been so stressed out about money that I can't think of anything else lately."

Stop, take a deep breath, and check your SUDS to see what has changed so far. Take note of any change and immediately start another round with a new modified Set-Up and Sequence.

2nd Set-Up:
"Even though I'm feeling a little better already, I still have a lot of stress, worry and anxiety over my lack of money and I don't know whether I'll ever have any money in my life. Yet, I love and accept myself no matter what happens."

2nd Sequence:
EB - "I'm feeling a little better already, but I still feel like I never have enough money - and life is difficult as a result!"
SE - "Why does this always happen to me!"
UE - "What can I do to change this? I'm not entirely helpless."

27

UN -"I feel like I must make some changes in my life to change this situation."

UM -"I'm afraid to make changes, but I need to make more money."

CB -"I am not helpless and I can make the changes necessary to change this situation."

UA -"I will do whatever it takes to find a job and start to make more money - now!"

TH -"I now make the choice to initially take whatever job I can find and then improve on it from there. Things will work out with time."

KC - "I may have been stressed out about money before this, but by knowing what to do and taking action, I'm sure things will change in my life and for my family now."

Stop, take a deep breath, and check your SUDS to see if anything has changed yet. Take note of any change and immediately start another round with a new Set-Up and Sequence.

3rd Set-Up:

"I'm feeling even better now about this entire issue and I now know that by changing my mind about things and taking action I will eventually have enough money to support myself or my family and I'm very happy about that."

"Even though I felt hopeless in the past, I now realize that I'm not helpless and things can get much better once I start taking action and follow through. And, yes, I feel like I do love and accept myself fully and completely."

3rd Sequence:

EB -"I'm feeling much better now and I know like this is going to work for me."

SE -"I've made a choice to change my life and things will get better now."

UE -"I know what I have to do and I know it will work for me. I'm not helpless any longer. I never was helpless."

UN -"I feel like I have changed already and things will get better."

UM -"I'm no longer afraid to make the changes in my life that are needed to make more money."

CB -*"I now realize I can make more money and I will start anywhere I must and move up from there."*

UA -*"I will do whatever it takes to earn more money for me and my family and be happy to do so."*

TH -*"I have already made the choice to change my life and now it's time to take action. Things will definitely work out now."*

KC - *"I know things have already changed and now I give it up to God and the Universe to make the rest of it happen. I remain available at all times to receive abundance."*

Stop, take a deep breath, and check your SUDS to see if anything is left that needs to still be addressed and if there is any part of the SUDS remaining, continue with the Set-Ups and Sequences until you are at a zero on your SUDS scale. Of course, change the words to fit your particular feelings as you continue tapping. Remember, the whole point of using words is to access the underlying negative feelings attached to the issue, so change the words or use inflections or volume in your voice to access the negative emotions to get the best results.

Panic Attacks

The term "Panic attack" is a psychological word that is commonly used by the general public. Since we don't do any diagnosis or specific treatment for psychological issues with EFT, we don't use that term to reflect a psychological diagnosis. We simply use the heading for those who recognize when they have so much anxiety, fear and stress that they can no longer be in control of their emotions and they often start to shake, cry or exhibit other uncontrollable traits. You may have been subject to what is known as a panic attack in common parlance or seen someone stressing out so much that other people became worried about their welfare to the point of interceding.

Such an extreme emotional "attack" can happen to anyone in the right (or wrong) circumstances, such as getting on an airplane and the fear of being in an enclosed space together with a fear of heights and perhaps the fear of being out of control all hit at once. When that happens, a person can begin screaming, crying, acting bizarrely, muttering to themselves or can exhibit almost any type of extreme behaviors.

Many people have called the Emergency Medical Services in their local area when this happens, but the most help they often get is to be given a brown paper bag and are told to breathe into it until they calm down. That just doesn't seem to be enough help in our opinion. When such an attack happens in a medical environment, the most doctors and nurses can do is give you a brown paper bag and a shot of Valium or something like that. Again, it's more like a band-aid than a solution.

On the other hand, EFT will calm people down when they are in extreme situations and it will often do it quite quickly. The first thing to remember when using EFT is to "KEEP TAPPING" yourself, a family member or friend throughout the entire event. It is not as important to use specific words with people who are going through a panic attack as to just KEEP TAPPING the entire time they are in it. That's because when they are experiencing such an extreme emotional outburst, you can be assured that their meridians are almost fully blocked and that's when you will get the best results using EFT.

For those who want some assistance in determining what words to use while doing the tapping, here are some Set-Ups and Sequences you may use when such an extreme emotional event occurs.

Set-Up preamble: As mentioned above, if a person is already in such an extreme situation, they are usually feeling their emotions fully already, so no formal Set-Up is needed. Instead, have them follow you through the tapping Sequence while you say the words for them or have them repeat them as best they can. But, just in case you need to focus their mind on the issue at hand, here are a series of Set-Ups and Sequences for you to use.

Set-Up:
"Even though I'm feeling overwhelmed with emotion, fear, anxiety and stress and I'm afraid (you may add or change any of these words as you see fit under the circumstances) I'm going to lose it any minute now, I'm doing the best I can, but I'm not sure how long I can hold it together."

"Even though I'm feeling so overwhelmed that I'm afraid I'm about to lose it, I love and accept myself fully and completely."

"I can't do this right now. I'm losing it - don't you understand? I don't want to do any stupid looking tapping either - leave me alone!"

Sequence: Remember - they may not want to or even be able to say any words after you say them, so if that happens, tell them to just listen to the words and focus their attention on them.

EB -"I can't do this right now! I'm overwhelmed!"
SE -"I can't believe this is happening to me!"
UE -"What am I supposed to do? I feel so helpless."
UN -"I feel like this tapping will never help me."
UM -"I'm so afraid right now!"
CB -"I'm so afraid and overwhelmed - nobody can help me."
UA -"Please help me, I'm afraid, but I feel totally lost at this point."
TH -"I feel like I'm completely out of control." (JUST KEEP GOING!)
EB - "I'm so stressed out right now."
SE -"It seems to be getting a little better now."
UE -"I'm still upset and distressed though and I still feel helpless."
UN -"I feel like this tapping may be helping me."
UM -"I'm not quite as afraid now."
CB -"I'm not as afraid and overwhelmed as I was."
UA -"Thank you, this seems to be helping. I'm still a little afraid, but it is getting better and better."
TH -"I feel like I'm coming out of it already and regaining control."
KC - "I'm not as stressed out about everything any more, I think this is working already and I like that."

Stop, take a deep breath, check your SUDS to see what has changed so far. Take note of any change and immediately start another round with a new modified Set-Up and Sequence.

2nd Set-Up:

"Even though I'm feeling a little better already, I still am worried that it might come back if I don't stay in control. But I am feeling better and I like that and just want this to all go away and I love and accept myself no matter what happens.

2nd Sequence:

EB -"I'm feeling a little better already, but I still feel like I need to regain control again."

EB - *"I believe this is leaving me now. I'm not so overwhelmed."*
SE - *"I can't believe it worked so fast for me!"*
UE - *"Wow! I'm really relieved, but now I'm afraid it will come back."*
UN - *"I feel like this tapping has really made a difference for me."*
UM - *"I'm still a little afraid it will return."*
CB - *"I now make a choice to let this fear go completely and realize that I am in full control of my emotions."*
UA - *"I feel much better already and know that I am in control of myself at all times now - even when I feel fear, I feel totally in control."*
TH - *"I feel like I'm completely in control again."*
EB - *"I feel so much better right now I can't believe it."*
SE - *"It seems like it never happened."*
UE - *"I'm no longer upset or distressed about anything."*
UN - *"I feel like this tapping has helped me immensely."*
UM - *"I'm not afraid any more."*
CB - *"I'm not afraid or overwhelmed at all now."*
UA - *"Thank you, it's over. I'm no longer afraid and I'm getting better and better."*
TH - *"I feel like I've regained my control."*
KC - *"I'm not stressed out about anything any more and I think this is working for me and I like that."*

Stop, take a deep breath, and check your SUDS to see if you're down to a one or zero or if it's higher than that. You should be feeling okay by this time with all the positive reinforcement wording included within the last Sequence. If necessary, start another round with a new Set-Up and Sequence, changing the words as needed to reflect your present feelings. Here is one final short Sequence to assist you if you have any reservations about whether the original feeling is completely gone.

Last Sequence:
EB - *"I feel much better now knowing that I'm finally in control again."*
SE - *"I feel like a weight has been lifted off my shoulders."*
UE - *"I feel lighter and free."*
UN - *"I feel so much better now, but I'm a little worried that when I stop, it might come back again."*
UM - *"I give up that fear now. It doesn't serve me and I no longer harbor it."*
CB - *"I know this relief is permanent and I like that a lot."*

UA -*"I am in control of my emotions and know that this change is permanent."*

TH -*"I made a choice to let go of all my old fears and I will not allow them back again. This has changed me completely."*

KC - *"I know I am different now and that nothing can ever take my internal control away from me again. I have no fears that can ever incapacitate me again. I feel great!"*

Stop, take a deep breath, and check your SUDS to see if anything is left that still needs to be addressed. If not, then you are finished. If there is anything left of your SUDS, continue using any or all of the Set-Ups and Sequences again until you are at a zero on your SUDS scale. Of course, change the words to fit your particular feelings if you continue tapping. Remember, the whole point of using words is to access the underlying negative feelings attached to the issue, so if you or someone else is already feeling their emotions strongly, you can simply tap on them while they feel those emotions instead of saying the words.

I'm Afraid it May Come Back Again

It's not unusual that once a fearful and stressful issue is resolved, that they begin to fear that once they stop tapping, it will all come back again. Here is a Set-Up and Sequence to address that issue.

Set-Up: (continuous tapping on KC)
"Even though I'm feeling much better now, I'm beginning to get worried that it will come right back again as soon as we stop, but I love and accept myself no matter what happens."

"Even though I know that makes no sense whatsoever, I'm still feeling a little fear, but I'm doing the best I can nonetheless."

"Why do I have to fear anything now that it's over? I feel great, so why do I need to fear anything? Yet, I still have this nagging feeling that it could all come back again."

1st Sequence: (tapping 5-7 times on each meridian access point)

EB - "I'm feeling so much better, but I'm feeling a little fear it will come back once we stop."

SE - "I can't believe it went away so fast!"

UE - "What if it all comes back again? I'm feeling a little worried."

UN - "I feel like this tapping is so strange that it just distracted me."

UM - "I'm worried that it's really not completely gone yet."

CB - "I've suffered so long from these, it's hard to accept that it's really gone for good."

UA - "It actually feels like it is gone for good and I'm very relieved."

TH - "I feel like I'm completely over it and I'm so thankful."

Stop, take a deep breath, check your SUDS to see what has changed so far. Take note of any change and immediately start another round with a new modified Set-Up and Sequence.

2nd Set-Up: (Continuous tapping on KC)

"Even though I'm feeling a lot less worried, I still have a little nagging fear it could come back and I love and accept myself no matter what happens.

"Even though I'm actually feeling much better and the fear is very reduced, I've had these attacks for so long, it seems inconceivable that they could be all gone so quickly. Yet, I love and accept myself no matter what happens.

2nd Sequence: (tapping 5-7 times on each meridian access point)

EB - "I'm feeling a lot better about this whole thing and that little nagging fear is leaving me now."

EB - "I now the fear is leaving me now. I'm a lot less fearful now."

SE - "I can't believe it worked so fast for me!"

UE - "Wow! I'm really feeling better and I like that a lot."

UN - "I feel like this tapping has really made a big difference for me."

UM - "I'm sure it is gone for good and I have no more fear about it."

CB - "I now realize this EFT really works and I'm happy it worked for me."

UA - "I feel so much better already and I have no more fear about it ever returning, knowing that if it ever should, I now know what to do about it. I truly feel totally in control."

TH - "I feel no more fear and am sure it is completely gone."

Stop, take a deep breath, and check your SUDS to see if you're down to a one or zero or if it's higher than that. You should be feeling okay by this time with all the positive reinforcement wording included within the last Sequence. Only if necessary, should you start another round with a new Set-Up and Sequence, changing the words as needed to reflect any further fears. You should find that all fear is gone and you're feeling fine.

Fear Involving Love and Sexual Issues

Many people are afraid to fall in love for fear of either being hurt or of hurting someone else. When this happens, they are often relegated to "standing on the sidelines" watching others in their family and friends going through relationships as they look on in longing or in judgment.

These fears about love and the potential for heartache often start during their earliest years and then grow in strength as they see families break up or spouses die leaving behind loved ones with broken hearts. This only cements their fears about ever entering into a love relationship and they become more distant from the prospect of ever falling love. Unfortunately, they can sometimes get so deeply entrenched in their thoughts and fears about love that they never break out of them and live out their lives alone and lonely.

Here are the Set-Up and Sequences to help remove those fears.

I'm Afraid to Fall in Love

First set your SUDS on your issue revolving around being afraid to go into enclosed spaces and then start with the Set-Up as follows:

1ˢᵗ Set-Up: (While tapping continuously on the KC point)
"Even though I'm afraid to fall in love, I miss having someone in my life to share my heart with and to have to love. Yet, I'm doing the best I can just to get through my life."

35

"I can't allow myself to fall in love. I'm too afraid I'll get hurt or end up with a broken heart and I don't love or accept myself either."

"It feels to me like falling in love will only lead to heartache and pain, so I'd rather avoid it later by avoiding love now. Yet, I'm doing the best I can to feel something for somebody because I'm tired of being alone and lonely."

1ˢᵗ Sequence: (tap 5-7 times on each point as you say the words below)
EB - *"I don't want to fall in love."*
SE - *"It never works out for anyone, so it will never work for me."*
UE - *"I've seen my friends and family fail at love so I'd rather not try."*
UN - *"Every time I think of being in love I get a terrible feeling in my stomach that tells me to stop before it's too late."*
UM - *"I can't even consider falling in love."*
CB - *"I don't feel worthy having anyone else love me."*
UA - *"I avoid possible loving relationships because I'm afraid of the outcome being bad."*
TH - *"I just bring myself to be vulnerable with another person."*
KC - *"I'm so stressed out over this that just thinking about love freaks me out."*

Stop, take a deep breath, and check your SUDS to see what, if anything, has changed so far. Take note of any change and immediately start another round with a new modified Set-Up and Sequence that addressed how you're feeling.

2ⁿᵈ Set-Up:
"Even though I'm feeling a little less stressed right now about the prospect of falling in love, it doesn't seem like it will ever be possible for me, yet, I'm doing the best I can under difficult conditions."

"Every time I get to thinking about someone to love, my stomach does flip-flops and I feel queasy and I think about something else, yet I really do want someone else in my life to love."

"I'm afraid if I allow myself to fall in love, it won't work out because I feel unworthy of being loved by anyone else and so I'd rather not even try."

2nd Sequence:

EB - *"I'm actually feeling a little less stressed out about my fear of falling in love."*

SE - *"I still don't think this is going to work for me, but I'm feeling a little better."*

UE - *"I'm surprised I can feel anything at all."*

UN - *"I'm still afraid to have any kind of loving relationship."*

UM - *"I'd like to at least give it a try. I've been lonely a long time."*

CB - *"I am still afraid someone else will judge me when they get to know me better. I'm afraid of that."*

UA - *"I really wish I could allow myself to fall in love. I'll be it would be great."*

TH - *"I still feel afraid to fall in love - but not as much as before."*

KC - *"I'm feeling a little less stressed about the prospect of falling in love and I like that a lot."*

Stop, take a deep breath, and check your SUDS to see if anything has changed yet. Take note of any change and immediately start another round with a new Set-Up and Sequence

3rd Set-Up:

"Even though I'm feeling better and a lot less stressed about falling in love, I'm still a little concerned what will happen if I allow myself to be vulnerable. Yet, I want to share with another person and just be myself."

"Now, when I think about falling in love, my stomach is fine and I'm starting to look forward to it instead and I love and accept myself better now."

"I'm feeling much more relaxed about sharing my life with someone else and I feel good about it."

3rd Sequence:

EB - *"I'm actually feeling a lot less stressed by the thought of having a loving relationship in my life and actually falling in love."*

SE - *"I now realize if I let down my defenses, someone who loves me will not necessarily hurt me and can love me just the way I am."*

UE - *"I'm feeling much better about this whole loving thing."*

UN -"I'm going to allow myself to feel love and to be loved."
UM -"Whatever happens - happens, but I've still enjoyed loving and being loved. I've been lonely too long."
CB -"I am not going to let my fears stand in the way of having love in my life any longer."
UA -"I know I am a loving person and I have much to offer to another."
TH -"I don't feel afraid to fall in love any more."
EB -"I'm willing to allow myself to fall in love."
SE -"I now choose to open up my heart and let love flow out to another."
UE -"I know that by giving love to another I am more likely to receive it back."
UN -"I'm willing to be vulnerable and not attached to the outcome."
UM -"Whatever happens when I love someone else is complete in giving the love and I expect nothing in return."
CB -"I am going to myself love another with no expectation that they must love me back to make it complete."
UA -"I know I can love someone else and that is enough."
TH - "When they also love me, it can be even sweeter, but it is not necessary for me to love them."
KC - "I now commit myself to love others and allow that to be enough for me and if they return my love then that's great too, but I am not attached to the outcome any longer."

Stop, take a deep breath, and check your SUDS to see how it has changed. You may find that you are much more open to loving others - without any need for them to love you back and a great deal of freedom comes from such a feeling. It also eliminates most fear. Just remember not to be attached to the outcome of any loving relationship into which you enter and love in the present moment and it will be much easier for you to fall in love.

If you feel the need to continue to tap on this issue (because for some people this is a huge issue) then go back to the Set-Up and Sequence that most appeals to your personal issues and tap again and again until they are gone. Take a deep breath and start another round with a new Set-Up and Sequence. Continue until your SUDS is at a zero.

Sexual Issues

While love and sex are usually intimately tied together, sometimes people don't connect the two and just approach sex on its own. Many more people suffer from sexual stress than might be apparent from outward appearances. Most people are too embarrassed to even discuss their sexual problems with their spouse, let alone anyone else. Sexual issues, fear, lack of knowledge or experience with sex tend to remain in the shadows and are very stressful for many people. This often causes a lot of dysfunction and additional stress in their lives and the lives of their spouse/partner as well as family members. When someone suffers from stress about sex, it can have profoundly negative effects upon their entire life.

We're going to run through a few sexually related issues to help you reduce your stress around sex. If the topic presented doesn't exactly fit your feelings about it, simply change the words to fit your situation and tap along with the Set-Ups and Sequences.

I'm Too Frightened to Have Sex

First set your SUDS on your issue revolving around being unemployed and then start with the Set-Up as follows:

1st Set-Up:
"Even though I think about sex often/sometimes, I am far too frightened to have sex with anyone. Yet, I love and accept myself nonetheless."

"Even though I love my partner, I'm too frightened to have sex because of all the negative things I've heard about it all my life. Yet, I'd like to try it nonetheless."
"Even though I am frightened of having sex - even with the one I love - I cannot even consider it because I am to scared. Yet, I love and accept myself nonetheless."

"Even though I am really curious about sex, I am too frightened to actually engage in sex with anyone because I'm sure I'll get too

stressed out just thinking about it and I'm very frustrated about the whole thing and I can't sleep at night as a result, but I'm doing the best I can to deal with this fear of sex."

1st Sequence:
EB - "I'm too afraid to have sex with anyone else."
SE - "I can't have sex with anyone else because I am frightened."
UE - "I wouldn't know what would to do if I tried."
UN - "I would feel mortified if tried and failed."
UM - "This is crazy! What do I have to be afraid about?"
CB - "I want to enjoy sex with my loved one, but I just can't do it -yet!"
UA - "Where do I turn for help? Who can I trust?"
TH - "I feel like I'm going to remain a virgin all my life. I'm too afraid to even try."
KC - "I'm so stressed out about all this that I can't think of anything else lately."

Stop, take a deep breath, and check your SUDS to see what, if anything, has changed so far. Take note of any change and immediately start another round with a new modified Set-Up and Sequence that addressed how you're feeling.

2nd Set-Up:
"Even though I'm feeling a little less frightened about sex, I'm still pretty frustrated and worried that I may remain a virgin for the rest of my life. Yet, I love and accept myself no matter what happens.

2nd Sequence:
EB - "I'm actually feeling a little better already, but I still feel frightened about just the thought of having sex with anyone else."
SE - "Why didn't I let this go a long time ago?"
UE - "Why can't I let this go now? I'm not completely afraid of sex."
UN - "I feel like there is something wrong with me when it comes to sex."
UM - "I'm afraid I'll do the wrong thing and look like a fool."
CB - "I am not about to make myself look like a fool. I'd rather remain a virgin."
UA - "No, I don't want to remain a virgin. I want to be able to enjoy sex naturally."

TH -*"I must make the choice to release this fear and return to my natural feelings which include sexual thoughts - without fear, shame or guilt. Things will work out for me with time."*

KC - *"I may have been frightened about having sex before this, but I am already releasing it and returning to my natural feelings about sex - without guilt, shame or fear."*

Stop, take a deep breath, and check your SUDS to see what has changed so far. Take note of any change and immediately start another round with a new Set-Up and Sequence.

3rd Set-Up:

"I'm feeling much more relaxed now about having sex. I don't feel as much fear, shame or guilt and feel like this issue is going to leave me completely - soon.

"Even though I felt frightened initially, I'm feeling much better now about the whole topic and realize it was all in my head and I can overcome these unnatural thoughts and enjoy a healthy sex life from now on and I love and accept myself fully and completely."

3rd Sequence:

EB -*"I'm feeling much better about sex and don't feel frightened any longer."*

SE -*"But now I'm a little worried that as soon as I stop this tapping, my fears will return again."*

UE -*"I now know what I have to do and I know it will work for me. I'm not a helpless victim any longer. I realize I never was helpless."*

UN -*"I feel like these fears have vanished from me already and things will get better now."*

UM -*"I'm no longer afraid to have sex and feel happy about that fact."*

CB -*"I now realize I can naturally have sex if I wish without guilt and recriminations and enjoy it."*

UA - *"I still have a small fear that I will overreact now and lose my morals, but I'm sure that's just my mind working on me."*

TH - *"I let all remaining fears and worries go about having sex and know that it can be a fulfilling experience without guild or shame."*

KC -*"I let all remnants of shame and guilt go and allow myself to enjoy sex in a joyful and exuberant way."*

KC - *"I know this fear has now changed and I give it up to God to allow me full freedom to engage in and enjoy sex without guilt or shame."*

Stop, take a deep breath, and check your SUDS to see if anything is left that needs to still be addressed and if there is any part of the SUDS remaining, continue with the Set-Ups and Sequences until you are at a zero on your SUDS scale. Of course, change any words to fit your particular feelings as you continue each round of tapping. Remember, the whole point of using words is to access the underlying negative feelings attached to the issue, so change the words or use different inflections or increase the volume in your voice to access the negative emotions to get the best results.

4th Set-Up:

"I'm feeling a lot better already about the thought of having sex and know things are going to work out for me in this area of my life and I love and accept myself fully and completely."

"I'm now feeling much more relaxed about the whole subject and realize I have been holding myself back for no good reason, other than the guilt and shame my parents imbued me with - which no longer applies to me and I now love and accept myself fully and completely."

"The whole idea of sex no longer repulses me and I'm feeling a new freedom in that area of my life - without guilt or shame and a new openness is arising within me to sharing my love physically."

4th Sequence:

EB - *"I'm feeling much, much better about the whole idea of sex being a natural part of my life as I let go of the old programming my parents taught me as a child."*

SE - *"I don't need that old programming any longer and I give it up thankfully."*

UE - *"I am now willing to move on with my life and take the issue of sex in stride and not overreact as I used to do."*

UN - *"I now choose to accept that I am entitled to have sex without fear, shame or guilt as a natural part of being a human being."*

UM -"If God gave me my body, why should I deny the use of it for the purpose for which it was intended?

CB -"If S/He didn't want me to have sex, S/He would not have given me sex organs and a desire within me to do so."

UA -"Sex is a natural part of my life which I intend upon enjoying."

TH -"I now choose to let go of any remaining fears and enjoy sex."

KC -"I now realize I've been making too much of this whole thing and I now choose to make a different choice about how I feel about sex."

KC - "I know that sex is a natural part of life and I'm going to be able to enjoy it from now on without guilt, shame or fear."

Stop, take a deep breath, and check your SUDS to see if anything has changed yet. Take note of any change and immediately start another round with a new Set-Up and Sequence.

I'm Afraid of Certain Sex Acts Because I've Been Taught They're Wrong

First set your SUDS on your issue revolving around being ashamed or guilty about doing certain sex acts which you think are wrong and then start with the Set-Up as follows:

1st Set-Up:

"Even though I'm afraid to do certain sex acts because I've been taught they're dirty and wrong, I love and accept myself nonetheless."

"Even though I am a good girl, and good girls don't do those nasty things with men - even with the one I love - I cannot even consider it because I am also scared. Yet, I love and accept myself nonetheless."

"Even though I am really curious about certain sex acts, I am too frightened to actually engage in them with anyone because I'm sure I'll go to Hell, yet, but I'm still curious and I'm doing the best I can to deal with my frustrations."

1st Sequence:

EB - *"I'm not willing to do certain things because they're wrong."*

SE - *"I can't do certain sex acts because I've been taught they're dirty and shameful."*

UE - *"I wouldn't know what would to do even if I want to try."*

UN - *"I would feel mortified if I messed it up."*

UM - *"What am I saying? I don't want to do those dirty things!"*

CB - *"I still am curious and I want to enjoy an active and varied sex life with the one I love, but I just can't do it -yet!"*

UA - *"Where can I turn for help? Who can I trust to ask?"*

TH - *"I feel like I'm going never going to enjoy my sex life."*

KC - *"I'm so stressed out over all this that I feel like it will never change."*

Stop, take a deep breath, and check your SUDS to see what, if anything, has changed so far. Take note of any change and immediately start another round with a new modified Set-Up and Sequence that addressed how you're feeling.

2nd Set-Up:

"Even though I'm feeling a little less worried about doing certain things with sex, I'm still pretty ashamed that I'm even asking about it. I may never experience any of those things I've heard about and be frustrated all my life. Yet, I love and accept myself no matter what happens.

2nd Sequence:

EB - *"I'm actually feeling a little better about this issue already, but I still feel frustrated and don't know who I can talk to about it."*

SE - *"Why didn't I just go ahead and do it a long time ago?"*

UE - *"Why can't I let go of my shame and fear now? I'm not completely afraid of sex and this is just part of it, isn't it?"*

UN - *"I feel like there is something wrong with me when it comes to different types of sex acts."*

UM - *"I'm afraid I might do it wrong and then look like a fool."*

CB - *"I am still too ashamed and guilty to even talk about this with anyone."*

UA - *"No, I don't want to stay this way. I will take a chance. I want to enjoy sex naturally."*

TH -"I now choose to experiment, and as long as I like it I'll continue."
KC - "I may have been frightened about having this different type of sex before, but I am already releasing it and returning to my natural feelings about sex - without guilt, shame or fear."

Stop, take a deep breath, and check your SUDS to see if anything has changed yet. Take note of any change and immediately start another round with a new Set-Up and Sequence.

3rd Set-Up:

"I'm feeling much better and more relaxed now about different sex acts and I don't feel as much fear, shame or guilt as I did before. I now feel like this issue is going to leave me completely.

"Even though I felt frightened and fearful initially, I'm feeling much better now about the whole topic and realize it was all in my head and I can now overcome those unnatural thoughts and enjoy a full and healthy sex life from now on and love and accept myself fully and completely too.

3rd Sequence:

EB -"I'm feeling much better about different types of sex acts and don't feel frightened any longer."

SE - "I now know I can let go of this issue entirely and enjoy all kinds of sex - if I want to."

UE - "I now know what I have to do and I know this will work for me. I'm not a helpless little child, but a grown adult and I have a right to enjoy my sex life the way I want to enjoy it."

UN -"My fears have vanished and things are already getting better."

UM -"I'm no longer afraid to have whatever type of sex I want and I am happy about that fact."

CB - "I now realize I can naturally enjoy having any kind of sex I wish without guilt and recriminations."

UA - "I release any remaining fears and embrace my sexual freedom."

TH - "I let all remaining fears and worries evaporate about having sex and know that it will be a fulfilling experience without guild or shame."

KC - "I remove all remnants of shame and guilt and allow myself to enjoy sex in a joyful and exuberant way -whatever way I choose."

KC - "I know that God allows me the full freedom to engage in and enjoy any type of sex - without guilt or shame."

Stop, take a deep breath, and check your SUDS to see if anything is left that needs to still be addressed and if there is any part of the SUDS remaining, continue with the Set-Ups and Sequences until you are at a zero on your SUDS scale. Of course, change any words to fit your particular feelings as you continue each round of tapping. Remember, the whole point of using words is to access the underlying negative feelings attached to the issue, so change the words or use different inflections or increase the volume in your voice to access the negative emotions to get the best results.

Additional issues of interest in the sexual area are listed below to give you more issues to consider and tap on until they are eradicated completely. Remember to change the words to fit your particular issues so you feel them completely while tapping. By doing this, you will get much better results. By the end of tapping on all these issues and whatever others you may feel, you will find that you and your loving partner will enjoy your sex life much more than ever before.

You may also wish to tap along with your partner on these issues until both of you are without any self-limiting beliefs about sex.

Additional sexual issues:
I'm so afraid of being hurt if I am vulnerable.
I'm too embarrassed to have sex with anyone else:
I'm so afraid of sexually transmitted disease that I won't have sex.
I'm afraid I don't know what to do when it comes to sex.
If sex is natural, why doesn't it seem that way to me?
I'm afraid sex is dirty and wrong.

Family Issues

While most people love their spouse and the members of their family, many have deeper problems and feel a great deal of stress from within their family. The irony is their home doesn't feel safe and secure, but has become a place of constant stress and difficulty. They want to find a solution, but don't know where to turn or how to find their way through the mess their lives have become.

I Love My Family, but Sometimes I Can't Stand Them

First set your SUDS on your issue revolving around being stressed when you are with family and then start with the Set-Up as follows:

1ˢᵗ Set-Up: (While tapping continuously on the KC point)
"Even though I love my family, there are times when they really annoy me and I want nothing to do with them, yet I'm doing the best I can and that's all I can do."

"Sometimes my family can really piss me off and then I feel guilty about that feeling because I know I really love them, yet, I'm doing the best that I can nonetheless."

"Even though I really want to just love them all the time, there are times when they can provoke me more than anyone else in the world - and then I feel guilty, but I love and accept myself no matter how I may feel about them from time to time."

1ˢᵗ Sequence:
EB - "I really love my family."
SE - "But there's nobody who can provoke me more than them."
UE - "I don't want to hate them, but that's the way it feels"
UN- "I know I always love them, but it's hard sometimes to remember when things aren't going well."
UM - "I feel so guilty feeling anything but love for them."
CB - "I love 'em, but I hate 'em."
UA - "It isn't supposed to be like this."
TH - "I feel so guilty even saying these words, but it's how I feel sometimes."
KC - "I just can't take all the pressure and stress sometimes."

Stop, take a deep breath, and check your SUDS to see what, if anything, has changed so far. Take note of any change and immediately start another round with a new modified Set-Up and Sequence that addressed how you're feeling.

2nd Set-Up (while continuously tapping the KC spot)

"I'm feeling so stressed being part of this family that it makes me crazy sometimes."

"I'm feeling a little less stressed now, but I know I'm going to have to go back into that family life again and that only stresses me out some more, but I'm going to do the best I can no matter what happens."

2nd Sequence:

EB - *"I'm actually feeling a little less stressed out right now than I was before."*
SE - *"I still have these terrible feelings about some of my family"*
UE - *"I feel like I love 'em and I feel like I hate 'em."*
UN - *"This is all so stressful and now I feel guilty too."*
UM - *"I'm doing the best I can under difficult conditions."*
CB - *"I forgive myself for harboring these conflicting thoughts."*
UA - *"I really love my family and I just don't do well with stress."*
TH - *"I know this will work its way out, but now I feel guilty."*
KC - *"I now choose to let go of all remaining guilt and stress and shame and just love my family for all I'm worth."*

3rd Sequence:

EB - *"I no longer need feel guilty or ashamed."*
SE - *"These feelings are normal in any family."*
UE - *"It's just how people feel for awhile and then they go back to loving one another again."*
UN - *"It's not permanent and there is nothing to be upset about."*
UM - *"I now choose to focus all my attention on loving and respecting my family no matter what happens or what they do."*
CB - *"I forgive myself for feeling that way in the first place."*
UA - *"I truly love my family and those negative feelings are now gone forever."*
TH - *"I let all negative thoughts go and focus on the love alone."*
KC - *"I now choose to let go of all remaining guilt and stress and shame and just love my family for all we're worth. We're in this together for the long run."*

Stop, take a deep breath, and check your SUDS to see if anything has changed yet. Take note of any change and immediately start another round with the 3rd Set-Up and Sequence.

3rd Set-Up:

"I'm now feeling a lot better about this fear of death and I make the commitment to let it go completely and permanently no matter what happens."

3rd Sequence:

EB - *"I'm actually feeling much better now and I let go off all vestiges of that fear now."*

SE - *"I now choose to give up any remaining fear and commit myself to life from this day forward."*

UE - *"I feel much better about this whole thing."*

UN - *"I no longer hold on to any remaining fear of death or dying."*

UM - *"I'm no longer afraid of death and focus my attention on life."*

CB - *"I now realize I never had anything to fear and it was just my mind pushing me into fear for no good reason."*

UA - *"I forgive my mind for its misunderstanding and fear."*

TH - *"I now realize this stress I was feeling was irrational and I permanently relinquish it so that it will not return."*

KC - *"I now choose to live my life to the fullest and live each day of my life in presence."*

Stop, take a deep breath, and check your SUDS to see what has changed so far. Take note of any change and immediately start another round with a new Set-Up and Sequence.

The following are additional examples of family issues and stressors you may experience. If any of them jump out at you and you feel you want to do EFT on them, use the Set-Ups and Sequences from any of the full sets and simply change the words as you need them to address your issue.

I can't really show my feelings with my family.
I feel distant from the certain members of my family at times.
I sometimes feel like a stranger in my own home.
I have secrets that I keep, especially from my family members.

49

Health Issues

Many people have health issues. Some admit them openly and seek assistance from health care professionals and their family, while others hide how they feel or are worried about showing how they really are fearful of losing friendships or their place in the hierarchy of their family or business.

I'm Afraid I'm Going to Die

First set your SUDS on your issue revolving around being ashamed or guilty about doing certain sex acts which you think are wrong and then start with the Set-Up as follows:

1ˢᵗ Set-Up: (While tapping continuously on the KC point)
"Even though I'm afraid I'm going to die anytime, I love and accept myself nonetheless."

"I'm always afraid I might die any time now, yet, I'm doing the best that I can nonetheless."

"Even though I'm really afraid to die, I'm doing the best that I can and that's all I can do for now."

1ˢᵗ Sequence:
EB - *"I'm really afraid to die."*
SE - *"I just can't get it out of my head."*
UE - *"I don't want to die, I'm afraid."*
UN - *"I know everyone dies at some time, but I don't want to!"*
UM - *"Just thinking about dying makes me nervous."*
CB - *"I can't seem to think of anything else other than dying and it's freaking me out."*
UA - *"This all started when I lost a relative/friend and experienced such a deep sense of loss and helplessness."*
TH - *"I feel like it is going to happen to me any time now."*
KC - *"I just can't get it out of my head that I'm going to die."*

Stop, take a deep breath, and check your SUDS to see what, if anything, has changed so far. Take note of any change and immediately start another round with a new modified Set-Up and Sequence that addressed how you're feeling.

2nd Set-Up: (while continuously tapping the KC spot)
"I'm feeling a little better already, but I know I'll die someday and that's still freaking me out."

"I'm a little less stressed than when we started, but I don't think I'll ever completely lose this fear of mine."

2nd Sequence:
EB - "I'm actually feeling a little less stressed out by the whole idea of dying because I realize it's going to happen to all of us."
SE - "Yet, I still have this unreasonable fear that comes up every once and awhile."
UE - "I feel like this fear and stress is lessening a bit."
UN - "I feel better about it now, but I'm not sure it will stay gone yet."
UM - "I'm still a little worried that my fear of death could get worse again."
CB - "I forgive myself for harboring this fear when I know it is unreasonable."
UA - "I now choose to let go of my fear of death."
TH - "I now make the decision to permanently let go of this fear of death and learn to live again as fully as possible."
KC - "I now choose to let go of all remaining fear and stress about being afraid of speaking in public."

Stop, take a deep breath, and check your SUDS to see if anything has changed yet. Take note of any change and immediately start another round with the 3rd Set-Up and Sequence.

3rd Set-Up: (while continuously tapping the KC spot)
"I'm now feeling a lot better about this fear of death and I make the commitment to let it go completely and permanently no matter what happens."

3rd Sequence: (tap 5-7 times on each point as you say the words below)

EB - *"I'm actually feeling much better now and I let go off all vestiges of that fear now."*

SE - *"I now choose to give up any remaining fear and commit myself to life from this day forward."*

UE - *"I feel much better about this whole thing."*

UN - *"I no longer hold on to any remaining fear of death or dying."*

UM - *"I'm no longer afraid of death and focus my attention on life."*

CB - *"I now realize I never had anything to fear and it was just my mind pushing me into fear for no good reason."*

UA - *"I forgive my mind for its misunderstanding and fear."*

TH - *"I now realize this stress I was feeling was irrational and I permanently relinquish it so that it will not return."*

KC - *"I now choose to live my life to the fullest and live each day of my life in presence."*

Stop, take a deep breath, and check your SUDS to see if anything has changed yet. Take note of any change and immediately start another round with a new Set-Up and Sequence.

These are some additional examples of types of fears and stressors you may experience. If any of them jump out at you and you feel you want to do EFT on them, use the Set-Ups and Sequences from any of the full sets and simply change the words as you need them to address your issue.

Here they are:

I'm ill and I can't tell anyone.

I'm having these pains, but I'm afraid to tell anyone about them.

I'm have this pain, but I'm afraid to go see a doctor about it.

Nobody really cares about me - until I'm sick. No wonder I'm sick all the time.

Why is it always me that cares for everybody else, but nobody cares about me.

I'm afraid to get sick since I am the only breadwinner in the family.

What will happen to my family if I get sick.

The only time anyone pays any attention to me is when I'm sick.

I'm so stressed out emotionally, I'm starting to feel physically ill.

Anger and Rage Issues

Anger and rage are being felt more often as our society becomes more complex and many people feel like their voice isn't heard or that others are unconcerned about them or are inconsiderate to them. When anger or rage are unexpressed, those emotions are often turned inward and that can lead to depression or other physical ailments. It is best to deal with anger and rage as early as possible in their cycle to avoid allowing them to fester within and perhaps have worse impact upon you.

"I Have a Lot of Road Rage"

First set your SUDS on your issue revolving around road rage and then start with the Set-Up as follows:

1st Set-Up: (While tapping continuously on the KC point)
"Even though I hate other drivers who cut me off or do inconsiderate things on the road, I love and accept myself nonetheless."

"I'm always judging other drivers because they're such idiots and so inconsiderate that I want to run them off the road, yet, I'm doing the best that I can to not do that."

"Even though I often feel like I want to ram other drivers' cars when they cut me off or do inconsiderate or dangerous things on the road, I'm doing the best that I can to avoid confrontations, but it is still very frustrating."

1st Sequence:
EB - *"I'm really frustrated by other drivers."*
SE - *"They are stupid and inconsiderate."*
UE - *"I hate stupid and inept drivers."*
UN - *"Some drivers drive too fast, while others drive to slow."*
UM - *"Nobody knows how to drive correctly but me."*
CB - *"Why are they such stupid drivers, while I'm the only good driver on the road?"*
UA - *"When are they going to learn how to drive?"*
TH - *"They are such idiots!"*

53

KC - *"It's so frustrating dealing with stupid drivers, but I'm doing the best I can to take them in stride."*

Stop, take a deep breath, and check your SUDS to see what, if anything, has changed so far. Take note of any change and immediately start another round with a new modified Set-Up and Sequence that addressed how you're feeling.

2nd Set-Up: (while continuously tapping the KC spot)
"I'm not feeling much better yet, because I know I'm going to have to drive again shortly and there will just be more stupid drivers out there waiting to make my life miserable again."

"I'm actually a little calmer now that I'm talking about all this and that makes me feel better, but I'm afraid I'm still going to get frustrated by other drivers again and I'm doing the best I can to deal with it."

"I'd actually like to let go of all this and start to just enjoy driving again."

2nd Sequence:
EB - *"I'm actually feeling a little less stressed out by the whole idea of driving with all those crazy nuts on the road."*
SE - *"I wonder if these feelings have anything to do with me?"*
UE - *"Maybe some of these feelings are a reflection of my judgments."*
UN - *"I'd like to let go of all my judgments and start to relax a bit."*
UM - *"How can I relax when all those idiots are still out there waiting to make me miserable again?"*
CB - *"I forgive myself for harboring these judgments of other drivers."*
UA - *"I now choose to let go of my judgments of other drivers, no matter how badly they drive."*
TH - *"If it wasn't for bad drivers, I wouldn't consider myself such a good driver."*
KC - *"It's just the duality of life showing up in my life."*

Stop, take a deep breath, and check your SUDS to see if anything has changed yet. Take note of any change and immediately start another round with the 3rd Set-Up and Sequence.

3rd Set-Up: (while continuously tapping the KC spot)

"I'm feeling a lot better about other drivers and now realize it has been my judgments that have been making me so upset and frustrated and I love and accept myself no matter what happens."

"I now choose to let those judgments go and start to recognize that every one has their own driving habits and nobody can dictate what anyone else does and I love and accept myself."

"I no longer need to judge everyone who is driving and try to teach them a lesson or do anything to them in response to their driving. I can choose peace and acceptance instead."

3rd Sequence: (tap 5-7 times on each point as you say the words below)

EB - *"I'm actually feeling much better now that I realize it's just my judgments that is making me so unhappy on the road."*

SE - *"I now choose to give up judging everyone else's driving habits and stay focused on my own driving and remain at peace instead."*

UE - *"I now feel much better about this whole issue."*

UN - *"I don't need to be upset all the time about how others drive."*

UM - *"It doesn't do me any good and it doesn't change how they drive."*

CB - *"I now realize I can drive without judging everyone else and just remain at peace instead and I like that idea."*

UA - *"I forgive my mind for being the judge - that's its job."*

TH - *"I now choose to take control and not be so judgmental and frustrated by other drivers and I will give them the benefit of the doubt from now on."*

KC - *"I now choose to drive without frustration or judgments and enjoy the ride much better without stress."*

Other issues you might want to tap on:

I hate inconsiderate people.

I feel like I have to get back at other drivers who disrespect me.

I hate commuting to work on the train and/or subway.

When someone embarrasses me, I want to hurt them.

When I get embarrassed, I want to hide.

When someone agrees to do something with me and then they don't do it, it really ticks me off.

When nobody will listen to me, I get really angry.
When I'm angry or enraged, you'd better not to come near me.

Fear Issues

Many people suffer from all kinds of fear and become stressed out over it because they don't believe there is any solution for their fears and they feel helpless. Fear undermines courage and dilutes self-esteem. Fear can take the form of almost anything, but mostly it has its roots in childhood when someone traumatized you and that trauma has stayed with you ever since in one form or another.

In public polls, it has been repeatedly reported that public speaking is the number 1 fear in the general public (that's right, it is even more fearful than death), so we're going to start with that.

Fear of Public Speaking

First set your SUDS on your issue revolving around being afraid to speak in public and then start with the Set-Up as follows:

1st Set-Up:(While tapping continuously on the KC point)
"Even though I'm afraid to speak in public places or events or even in front of small groups, I love and accept myself nonetheless."

"I can't speak in public because I'm afraid of messing up and feeling foolish. Yet, I love and accept myself fully and completely nonetheless."

"Even though I don't feel comfortable saying anything in front of people because I'm afraid I'll say the wrong thing and I'll feel like a fool, yet I'm doing the best that I can and that's all I can do for now."

1st Sequence:
EB -"I' can't talk in front of any group of people."
SE -"I just can't do it."
UE -"I don't want to speak in front of any type of meeting."
UN -"I'm afraid I'll feel foolish and make a fool out of myself."

UM - *"Just thinking about it puts me into a cold sweat."*
CB - *"I'm afraid it will never change and I'll always be afraid to try."*
UA - *"This all started when I was really young and I was embarrassed."*
TH - *"I feel like an idiot because I can't speak in front of even the smallest group of people."*
KC - *"I just can't do it no matter how small the group."*

Stop, take a deep breath, and check your SUDS to see what, if anything, has changed so far. Take note of any change and immediately start another round with a new modified Set-Up and Sequence that addressed how you're feeling.

2nd Set-Up: (while continuously tapping the KC spot)
"Even though I'm feeling a little less worried about talking in front of a group of people, I'm afraid I'll never really get used to speaking in public, yet I love and accept myself no matter what happens."

2nd Sequence:
EB - *"I'm actually feeling a little less stressed out by the whole concept of public speaking and I like that."*
SE - *"I still have this fear that I'll never be any good at public speaking."*
UE - *"I feel a little ashamed of myself."*
UN - *"I feel better about it, but I've tried it before and don't think I'll ever really get over this fear of public speaking."*
UM - *"I'm afraid I may never be able to talk in front of any size group."*
CB - *"Actually, I'm feeling better than I was before already."*
UA - *"I now choose to let go of my fear about public speaking."*
TH - *"I know this stress is lessening as we do this process."*
KC - *"I now choose to let go of all remaining fear and stress about being afraid of speaking in public."*

Stop, take a deep breath, and check your SUDS to see if anything has changed yet. Take note of any change and immediately start another round with the 3rd Set-Up and Sequence.

3rd Set-Up: (while continuously tapping the KC spot)
"Even though I'm now feeling a lot better about speaking I public in front of a group of people, I don't want to be left with any remaining

fear that could return later and I love and accept myself no matter what happens."

3ʳᵈ Sequence: (tap 5-7 times on each point as you say the words below)
EB -"I'm actually feeling much better about my prior fear and stress about any kind of public speaking and I like that."
SE - "Now I have a little fear that it may come back once I stop tapping,"
UE - "I feel a lot better already."
UN -"I no longer have anything to fear whenever I speak in public."
UM -"I'm no longer afraid to talk in front of any size group."
CB - "I now realize I have nothing to be ashamed of and all I have to do is stand up and speak as if there was only one person present and I'll do fine."
UA - "I now choose to be fine with any form of public speaking."
TH - "I now realize this stress was just an irrational fear that will not return."
KC - "I now choose to let go of any remaining fear or stress about this issue."

I Can't Go into Enclosed Spaces like an Elevator, Airplane or Anything like That

First set your SUDS on your issue revolving around being afraid to go into enclosed spaces and then start with the Set-Up as follows:
1ˢᵗ Set-Up: (While tapping continuously on the KC point)
"Even though I'm afraid to enter small, enclosed spaces, yet I love and accept myself nonetheless."

"I can't go into an elevator, airplane or small bathroom because I'm afraid I'll get stuck inside and never be able to get out. Yet, I love and accept myself fully and completely nonetheless."

"Even though I have tried many times to go into an elevator or airplane, I always feel like I'm out of control and will get caught inside and never get out. Yet, I love and accept myself no matter what happens."

1ˢᵗ Sequence: (tap 5-7 times on each point as you say the words below)

EB - *"I can't to go into an elevator no matter what."*

SE - *"I can't do it."*

UE - *"I wouldn't go into an elevator or into an airplane no matter what the consequences."*

UN - *"I would collapse if I went into either of them."*

UM - *"Whenever I even think about it, I go into a cold sweat."*

CB - *"I will never be able to go into an enclosed space, no matter how much I try."*

UA - *"Why do I have to go into such a place? I can't."*

TH - *"I feel like I'm never going to be able to go into a small space."*

KC - *"I'm so stressed out over all this and I feel like it will never change."*

Stop, take a deep breath, and check your SUDS to see what, if anything, has changed so far. Take note of any change and immediately start another round with a new modified Set-Up and Sequence that addressed how you're feeling.

2ⁿᵈ Set-Up:

"Even though I'm feeling a little less worried about going into an enclosed space and I'm tired of stressing out over it, yet I love and accept myself no matter what happens.

2ⁿᵈ Sequence:

EB - *"I'm actually feeling a little better about going into an enclosed space, but I'm still feel frustrated about it."*

SE - *"How did this happen to me?"*

UE - *"I feel a little better about all this."*

UN - *"I still have a little fear about going into enclosed spaces."*

UM - *"I'm afraid I may never be able to go into small spaces."*

CB - *"I am actually feeling better already."*

UA - *"I now choose to let go of all remaining fear about going into an elevator or airplane."*

TH - *"I know this terrible stress is about to leave me now."*

KC - *"I now choose to let go of all remaining fear and stress about being afraid of getting into an elevator or an airplane."*

Stop, take a deep breath, and check your SUDS to see what has changed so far. Take note of any change and immediately start another round with a new Set-Up and Sequence if you need it.

Fear of Heights

Many people are afraid of heights who are otherwise courageous and have no other obvious fears, but heights really scare them. This fear usually started when they were children and they were traumatized in some way and then it became a common fear for them. Ironically, many people who have such a fear wind up avoiding all kinds of things in their life, especially those things that have anything to do with high places. Here are the Set-Up and Sequences for it.

First set your SUDS on your issue revolving around being afraid to go into enclosed spaces and then start with the Set-Up as follows:

1st Set-Up: (While tapping continuously on the KC point)
"Even though I'm afraid of heights and don't like to go anywhere near the edge of high places, I love and accept myself nonetheless."

"I can't go anywhere near high places, I avoid them at all costs. Yet, I love and accept myself fully and completely nonetheless."

"Even though I want nothing to do with heights because of all my fear and it causes me all kinds of stress, I'm doing the best I can under difficult circumstances."

1st Sequence: (tap 5-7 times on each point as you say the words below)
EB -"I can't to go any where near high places."
SE -"I won't go near the edge of any overhang or ledge."
UE -"I wouldn't go to the top of a tall building - ever!"
UN -"I get a terrible feeling in my stomach when I get close to the edge of a tall building or any building."
UM -"I can't even look out of a window if I'm in a tall building."
CB -"This fear is so debilitating that I'm sure I'll never get over it."
UA -"I avoid going to the upper floors in any tall building."
TH -"I just can't do it."

KC - "I'm so stressed out over this fear of heights."

Stop, take a deep breath, and check your SUDS to see what, if anything, has changed so far. Take note of any change and immediately start another round with a new modified Set-Up and Sequence that addressed how you're feeling.

2nd Set-Up:
"Even though I'm feeling a little better about high places, and a little less worried about looking out of a window in a tall building, I love and accept myself no matter what happens."

2nd Sequence:
EB -"I'm actually feeling a little less stressed out about my fear of heights and that makes me feel much better already."

SE -"I still can't see myself going up on the roof of any building, but at least I'm not as afraid as I was before."

UE -"I'm actually feeling a little better about all this."

UN -"I still have a little fear left, but it seems to be changing."

UM -"I'm actually willing to give it a try now."

CB -"I am feeling much better about being in high places."

UA -"I now choose to let go of all remaining fear about high places and recognize that I can let this fear go now."

TH - "I am no longer stressed out by just the thought of being high and can envision myself being at ease in a tall building."

KC - "I now choose to let go of all remaining fear and stress about being afraid of heights."

A Story about How Things Happen According to Plan and Then Go Wrong and Then Can Change Again

Sometimes the best laid plans can go awry when you least expect it. I have run a weekly EFT Borrowing Benefits Group for nearly fifteen years and a number of students have chosen to use what they learn in the weekly groups to help them change their lives. One outstanding student recently made a conscious choice to sell her home and move out of state. She wanted less stress in her life and she felt by selling her three family home, she would eliminate the daily rigors of being a landlord as well as leave the rat race of New York City.

To her credit, once she made up her mind to sell her house, she almost immediately put in on the market and (true to the Law of Attraction) the Universe rewarded her steadfast belief that she would sell her house quickly with a qualified buyer. She entered into a contract which required her to evict the tenants in the house so that by the time the closing was held, it would be vacant for the new buyers. Everything was going along fine and being done right on schedule when (as I was in the midst of writing this book) she called me one Sunday afternoon and disclosed she was "freaking out." When I asked why, she responded that although she had made the decision to sell her house, now that it was actually happening and the first tenant had moved out and the second tenant was about to leave, she was suddenly worried whether she had done the right thing or not. Her mind was raising all kinds of thoughts, worries and fears and she was "freaking out!"

We immediately started an EFT session over the phone which went something like this:

1ˢᵗ Set-Up:(While tapping continuously on the KC point)
"Even though I'm freaking out because I can't believe this is all happening so fast and I'm not comfortable with the whole thing, I love and accept myself nonetheless."

"What did you do to me Ted? I listened to you and made up my mind to sell my house, but I never expected it to really happen this quickly and - I'm freaking out!"

"I knew I should never listen to you! What was I thinking? Selling my house is the dumbest thing I could ever do."

1ˢᵗ Sequence: (Tap 5-7 times on each point as you say the words below)
EB -*"I can't believe I actually did this to myself."*
SE -*"I'm freaking out."*
UE -*"I never expected this to all happen so quickly."*
UN -*"This is all feeling so real already."*
UM -*"I don't want to leave my home and my safety."*

CB - *"What was I thinking? I must have been crazy!"*
UA - *"Why did you talk me into all this in the first place?"*
TH - *"I feel like the world is coming down on me right now."*
EB - *"I can't believe this is happening already."*
SE - *"I know this was all my choice, but - I'm freaking out."*
UE - *"I never expected to feel this way about all this."*
UN - *"It all sounded so easy and simple, but that's not how it feels."*
UM - *"I'm feeling scared about the whole thing right now."*
CB - *"I knew what I was doing and I realize this is just my mind freaking out and it's going to be alright."*
UA - *"I did this because it was a good idea and it will work out."*
TH - *"I know this is going to all work out in the end."*
KC - *"I felt so stressed out at first, but I'm already feeling better and I now realize it was just my mind getting carried away."*

Before we had finished the entire double Sequence, I heard her yawn deeply and I knew the issue was almost gone. Yawning, stretching, taking a deep breath and other releases are a good way to tell when someone is letting go of their stress and feeling better. By the time we finished she was relieved and realized it was just her mind that had gotten carried away with itself and she felt much better and was ready to move forward. She didn't require another Sequence because she almost immediately came down from her "freaked out" status to a reasonable state of mind quickly. That was in large measure because she was sure the EFT would work for her and, more importantly, she was exhibiting a SUDS of 10 when we started and that's usually when the best results occur.

How to Handle Other Fears and Stressors

If you have fears about any of the following fears or stressors, continue to tap on any or all of the following issues, changing the words according to your own personal stressful feelings about them. Start by first setting your SUDS, do the Set-Up three times and then do the Sequence as many times as it takes to completely eliminate the entire SUDS on the issue. You'll find that the next issue arises naturally after that happens.

<u>Other Related Issues You May Wish to Tap On</u>:
I'm afraid to drive over bridges.
I'm afraid to drive on parkways.
I hate to go through tunnels.
I hate to fly.
When someone embarrasses me, I want to hurt them.
When someone embarrasses me, I want to run and hide.
I'm afraid of small animals.
I can't stand insects, spiders or snakes.
I hate frogs and rodents.
I'm afraid of mice or rats.
Dogs scare me a lot.
Small animals scare me.
Snails gross me out.
Spiders are very scary to me.
I'm afraid of being left alone.
I'm afraid to leave my house.
I'm afraid I'm not worthy of his/her love.
I'm afraid to love anyone else.
I'm not worthy of being abundant.
I'm afraid I don't have anything to offer anyone else.
Why would anyone want to love me?
I'm afraid of being taken advantage of again.
Everyone wants something from me.
All women want is money from me.
All men want is sex from me.

We're now going to move on to another way to not only eliminate the immediate stress you feel now, but all the stress that you have stored within your body from a lifetime of stress.

The Personal Peace Procedure

Once you've completed the stress portion of the book and feel most of your stress is resolved, you may want to continue the process by eliminating all the remaining stress from past events and people in your life. Those people and events tend to have an impact upon your present life because earlier incidents tend to leave "scars" in your emotional being (and your meridians) which then tend to influence how you react to certain situations that arise in life.

Those emotional scars can almost always be traced back to various people in your history who have done something to you that left that scar. It's almost like hearing a popular song from years ago brings up a particular memory of someone. A particular negative behavior is often triggered by the memory of a person in your past.

If you eliminate the memories and traumas associated with those people from your past, you can then eliminate the negative emotions associated with them and eliminate more of the stress in your life. When you eliminate all of those old memories, you'll live more of your life in peace and tranquility.

With the Personal Peace Procedure, we use EFT to eliminate those old memories and the people associated with them. The process is quite simple and straight forward and when you follow it to the letter, you'll discover that it works like a charm and before long you'll be feeling quite peaceful on many levels.

Since you've already eliminated many of the stresses you experience today, consider what your life could be like without all the emotional scars of your past weighing you down as well. If you could eliminate all of that old emotional baggage, what would your life be like? It would be great! That's what the Personal Peace Procedure is going to help you accomplish for yourself. By the time you're done with the procedure, you will know how to eliminate all the remaining negative feelings in your life so that your life can be peaceful, effortless and fun again.

Less stress translates into a higher degree of personal peace and far less emotional suffering. When you neutralize the remaining negative emotional baggage you carry around, you will be able to relate to the world better from a place of peace and you will feel better. That's what the Personal Peace Procedure will help you do.

Just as the elimination of stress, this process is based upon the basic premise of EFT which is that "all negative emotions, self-limiting beliefs, pain and aberrant behavior come from a blockage in your energy meridians." That includes all of your old emotional "stuff" that you carry around with you is really nothing more than a series of blockage in your energy meridians. As you already learned, energy meridians are little pathways which are located within the body which carry life force energy, known as "Chi." When the Chi is blocked, it results in all those negative emotions mentioned above. Once that is done, the underlying emotional issues that have held you back for so long will be eliminated and you'll feel emotionally free and at peace again.

Where to Start

This is where the real work begins. The Personal Peace Procedure is a process where you list every person or incident in your life that ever left you emotionally scarred or feeling like you are limited in any way. The reason you list them all is to give you a starting point from which to start with a Master List and then you can keep track while you are following the procedure.

Start your Master List from the present time and work your way backwards until you can't remember any more. If you don't find at least 50-300 people and/or incidents you are either going at it half-heartedly or you have led a sheltered life. Most people find hundreds. Some find thousands. It doesn't matter how many there are - it only matters that you list them all.

While making your Master List you may find that some people or events don't cause you any current discomfort. That's okay. List them anyway. The fact that you remember them suggests some remaining need for resolution.

66

Identify each person and then give each specific event a title as though it was a "mini-movie" like:

Examples: I Didn't Do it
                  I Can't Do this Anymore
                  Dad Beat Me Hard That Day
                  I Stole Suzie's Sandwich
                  Jimmy Stole My Bike
                  I Slipped and Almost Fell into the Grand Canyon
                  My Third Grade Class Ridiculed Me
                  Mom Locked Me in a Closet for 2 Hours Once
                  I Never Told Anyone What Mom Did to Me
                  Mrs. Adams Told Me I Was Stupid
                  Steve Hit Me with a Rock and Hurt
                  I Hate My Uncle for What He Did to Me, etc.

When your Master List is complete, pick out the most important issues to you, the "redwoods" in your "negative forest" of complaints, set a SUDS on each of them and use EFT on each of them until you either can't access the original feeling any more or you wind up laughing about it. Be sure to notice any aspects of each issue that may arise and work on each of them as separate "trees" in your "negative forest" of emotional issues. Continue to apply EFT to each and every issue until your SUDS is down to a zero on each one. Once it happens on the first issue, move on to the next issue by setting a SUDS on it and working on it with EFT until it is gone too.

The way the Personal Peace Procedure works is you continue to work on each issue until it is fully resolved and then move on to the next one. You continue to work on every name or incident on your Master List until they're all gone. It may take months to complete this process, but it will be well worth it by the time you're done. Once all people and incidents are gone, you are left in a neutral position and you will feel free again to enjoy your life - without any baggage hanging on to you.

If you cannot feel a SUDS intensity level on a particular topic or "mini-movie," then assume you are repressing it and apply as many rounds of EFT on it as it takes so that you are no longer feeling it at all.

After the big "redwoods" have been removed, move on down your Master List to the next "tree" and work on it until it is gone. Or you may also simply go to the next issue that naturally arises from your subconscious and work on it until it is resolved. Remember to always set a SUDS before starting so you know when you're done.

Do at least 3-5 people or mini-movies (specific event) per day, preferably 5, for 3 months. That should only take less than a half hour per day. At that rate you will have resolved nearly 500 specific events in 3 months. You will begin to notice how your body and mind feel better. You will likely notice how your "threshold for getting upset" starts to improve. Most amazing, your relationships will start to improve and how many of your deep emotional issues just don't seem to have the same power over you any longer. You may wish to revisit some of the specific events you listed on your Master List to see if they have any charge left to them after you've finished your first 3 months and you will likely notice how those previously intense incidences have faded into nothingness in your mind. Also take some time to notice any improvements in your blood pressure, pulse, eye sight and breathing ability. These are all things that can improve just by letting go of old "stuff" that was holding you back in the past.

Consciously notice these things because, unless you do, the quality healing you will have accomplished may be so subtle that you may not realize it. You may even dismiss it saying, "Oh well, that was never much of a problem for me anyway." This happens repeatedly with EFT and this is why it is brought to your awareness before you start the process.

If you are taking medications, you may feel the desire to discontinue some or all of them. If you choose to discontinue any medication ONLY do so after seeking a qualified physician's advice and approval. Follow their prescribed method for discontinuance since, with many medications, you must wean yourself off it slowly.

It is our sincere hope that the Personal Peace Procedure will become a worldwide routine for everyone. A few minutes each day for each student, teacher and principal will make a monumental difference in school performance, relationships, health, wealth and our overall quality of life throughout the world. Peace could make a big comeback.

More Questions That May Help to Trigger You

For those of you who are having a hard time remembering those people and/or events that have upset or scarred you, or those of you who may have hidden them away in the distant recesses of your mind, we have included a series of questions that may help you remember. You know, words, smells, sounds, songs and any number of other triggers that bring back all those old memories that you wish to avoid. Remember that the more of those negative emotions you can remember, the better the opportunity for you to heal them. **You have to feel them to heal them**. But you only need to feel or access them *for an instant* while you're tapping on them and then they're gone. Take your time with each question or prompt and let your mind freely associate. Get out a pad of paper or open up your computer and start to answer each question as you think about it. Even after you've finished the list, go back and do it again. You'll be surprised at how your memory will be jogged by many of the questions and later remember things you thought were completely gone. Make your list as complete as you can.

What words "trigger" you? List them.

What names "trigger" you? List them.

What emotions are "triggered" when you hear those words or names?

What incident, when it's thought of or mentioned, makes you upset, angry or some other negative emotion?

Which parent mistreated you the most? How?

Which sibling mistreated and/or teased you the most?

Which one of your friends teased or tortured you?

Who or what makes you feel fear and/or anxiety? List them and explain.

Were you ever lost of abandoned? By whom?

What actions of one or both of your parents most irritated you?

Which relatives irritated or upset you as a child?

Which relatives still irritate, upset or aggravate you?

Who betrayed you? List them.

Who betrayed your trust and caused you not to trust anymore?

Who has judged you? List them.

Who judges you now? List them.

What or who causes you to feel dis-empowered in any way?

Which teacher gave you the hardest time in grade school?

Were you ever embarrassed while you were in school? List them.

Did you ever get embarrassed during extra curricular activities?

Were you ever really frustrated by any specific experience during school or after school? List them.

Remember all of the embarrassing incidents during your school years? List them.

Which teacher gave you the hardest time in middle school?

Did you have acne while you were in middle school or high school?

Which teacher gave you a hard time in high school?

Did you ever fail a subject or a full year of school? How did it feel to you?

Did you ever have any nightmares from your fears of failing? How long did they last?

How about college? Who frustrated you there?

Any professor or teacher give you a particularly hard time during that period?

What about graduate school? Any anxieties related to it?

What about licensing examinations? Did you ever fail? How did you feel?

Did you ever have any friends who gave you a hard time or embarrassed you in any way? List them.

Was there ever a group of people you thought were cool and they rebuffed you? How did it make you feel?

Did you ever pledge for a high school or college fraternity or sorority and get hazed?

Who was the most demanding and/or demeaning person who hazed you?

Did you ever have a fight with anyone as you were growing up? List them.

Whether you won or lost, what emotions come up for you as soon as you think about those incidents?

Were you ever embarrassed by any of your brothers or sisters? List them specifically.

Did you ever really like somebody and they rebuffed your advances? List them.

Did anyone ever show an interest in you and you were offended by it? List them.

Did you ever try to get someone interested in you and you were frustrated because they didn't get it? List them and how it made you feel.

Were you ever asked out by someone and the date went well until a certain point and then went straight downhill and ended badly? List them.

Were you ever on a date and your date wanted something you weren't willing to deliver and they reacted badly?

Were you ever "date raped"?

Did you ever take advantage of a girl or woman sexually? How did that make you feel and how does it make you feel now?

Did you ever report it an assault or a rape and then have to be humiliated by the police, Doctors, Prosecutor, parents and everyone who found out? How did you feel?

Did you ever decide not to report a sexual assault because of your fears about all of the exposure it had for you and then later regretted it?

Did you ever have an abortion? How did that make you feel? How does it make you feel now?

Did you ever force anyone to have an abortion? How did that make you feel and how does it make you feel now?

Have you ever lost a child?

What losses in your life do you still grieve? List them.

Who do you still grieve? List them.

Do you have any remorse about anything or anyone?

Did you ever insult anyone else? Who? How did that make you feel?

Were you ever insulted by anyone else? Who? Under what circumstances? How did it make you feel? List the times and people.

Did you ever become outraged by someone? List them.

What smells incite you to feel emotions? Which ones? List them.

What chemical smells bring back bad memories for you?

What sounds bring out negative feelings for you? List them.

What songs bring back bad memories for you? List them and explain each.

What makes you sad?

Do you ever feel a profound sadness or sense of loss? What or who is that connected to?

Do you ever feel a profound sense of shame? What or who is that connected with? List them.

When you are hungry, does this ever "trigger" you? How?

When you are tired, does this "trigger" you? Explain.

Do you ever feel a profound sense of being alone or abandoned? What or who does that remind you of? List them.

When you are alone, do you ever feel abandoned or separate?

When you are lonely, what feelings arise within you?

When you get angry, who does that usually remind you of and why?

When you drive, what types of drivers most upset, disturb or anger you? List them and explain.

When you drive, what type of behavior upsets you? List them and explain.

When you are a passenger, what type of behavior most upsets you? Explain.

Do you ever find yourself judging others' intellect when they do something you deem stupid?

How do you feel when someone else does something that seems stupid to you?

Have you ever been told that you were stupid?

How did that make you feel? How does that make you feel now?

What is the worst thing that ever happened to you?

List other things that have happened to you that made you feel badly.

Have you ever hurt someone's feelings and regretted it later?

Who and what situations have ever caused you to feel guilty?

Have you ever been hurt and resented it? By whom? List them.

Does anyone's ineptitude upset you? If so, who? List them and explain.

Who or what circumstances have made you feel ashamed?

Has anyone ever been rude to you? List them and explain the circumstances.

Does arrogance annoy or anger you?

Who or what situations have ever made you feel threatened?

Who has ever been arrogant towards you or others in your presence? List them. How did it make you feel?

Has anyone ever been insolent towards you? Did it upset or anger you? List them.

Have any children ever frustrated or embarrassed you? List them and explain.

Have any children gotten into trouble and "triggered" your anger? List them.

Have any of your children or grandchildren frustrated you? List them.

Have any of your children ever let you down or embarrassed you? How? List them.

Have any grandchildren ever let you down or embarrassed you? How? List them.

Have any stepchildren ever upset you? If so, how and who?

Have your parents ever embarrassed you? If so, explain and list them.

Have any other relatives ever embarrassed you? List them.

Has your spouse or an ex-spouse ever embarrassed you upset you? List them.

Has an ex-boyfriend, fiancé or former girlfriend ever embarrassed you? List them. Have they ever frustrated you? Explain.

Have they ever taken advantage of you? List them.

When you are tired, what upsets you the most?

When you are lonely, what and/or who does it remind you of the most?

What just "pisses you off"?

Who just "pisses you off"?

Who do you harbor a grudge against? Who harbors one against you? Explain.

Who do you still resent today? List them.

Who still resents you today? List them.

Which ones still hurt you to think about? List them.

Who will you never forgive?

Were you ever embarrassed during a sporting event?

Every person who ever gave you a hard time, hurt you or upset you.

All the people you loved who broke up with you;

Anyone who ever embarrassed you in public;

Any employer who humiliated you or fired you;

Parents who disciplined you by hitting or spanking you;

Any fist-fight you've been in;

Any accidents you've ever been in;

Any time you've been arrested or in jail;

If anything has ever been stolen from you;

Anyone who has ever cheated you;

Anyone who has ever stolen your date or your loved one;

Any person who has ever taken advantage of you;

Anyone who has ever lied to you and hurt you;

Everyone who has ever hurt your feelings;

Anyone who has ever spoken badly about you behind your back;

Any time you've ever been physically injured;

Anyone who has ever sexually abused you;

Anyone who has done anything bad to you;

Anyone who has let you down (You may include God letting you down);

What physical problems do you have that keep you from being all you want to be?

Do you resent any part of that physical problem?

Are you angry for being ill? At whom?

Are you angry at God for anything? List them.

Do you feel like a victim?

Do you hate anyone? If so, list them and explain why.

Are you angry at anyone? If so, list them and explain why.

Is anyone angry at you? If so, why? How does that make you feel?

Does anyone hate you? If so, why? How does that make you feel?

Are there any other incidents that you've had in your life that haven't been elicited with the above questions that left you scarred in any way? If so, list them and explain why.

Every one of these names or descriptions of incidents should go onto your Master List which you will then use as previously explained. By the time you are finished with them all, your life will be transformed and you will be at peace.

Positive Affirmations

Once you've completed all of the negative elimination procedures, as mentioned above, you should find yourself with a decidedly positive and peaceful viewpoint. However, some people may find they feel as though they are left without many internal feelings at all. They may feel a void or absence of emotions.

If you'd like to infuse yourself with new, positive feelings to fill any void that may be left, we have included a series of positive affirmations that you can say while you tap on the <u>opposite</u> side of all your meridian access points. That is, as you recall, you've been using your dominant hand to do the tapping up until now to eliminate the negatives in your life. Now, to drive home the positive affirmations, you may want to switch to the non-dominant hand and tap the other side of your body's meridian access points as you repeat each positive affirmation phrase. If you've been tapping both sides of the meridian access points, then keep on doing exactly that and just follow the positive affirmations provided.

We call this "Choices" (as first described by Dr. Patricia Carrington) and we structure it by prefacing the positive affirmation with words to the effect of "I now <u>choose</u> . . . to feel safe and serene each and every day" or "It is my <u>choice</u> . . . to feel better about myself every day in every way" or "I choose . . ." By making choices, you are reaffirming that it is your choice to establish a more positive thought process in your life and reaffirm your personal power to make such choices in the present and in the future.

Here are a number of positive affirmations that you may use during this positive affirmation Choices segment. They are to be used once you honestly feel that you've eliminated <u>all</u> of the negative feelings within you. It is best to only infuse positive thoughts once you have eliminated the negatives completely. If you want to use positive affirmations as part of a "re-framing" technique where you turn the negative wording into positive wording, that's fine too, but always make sure you're completely finished with the negative side first before turning to the positive wordings.

You may notice that there are no Set-Ups mentioned in the positive affirmation segment. That is because it is no longer necessary because all of the positive affirmations are going to be directly infused into your subconscious mind as you tap each meridian access point.

As you continue to tap each of the meridian access points, say each phrase at <u>all</u> of the points for at least one full Sequence or, in some instances, you may choose to change phrases at each access point if the positive phrases are related to one another. However, it is important to say words to the effect of "**I now choose**" or "**It is my choice to** . . ." **_before_** each phrase so that you're making it into your choice to embrace this new positive mind set upon yourself.

We suggest you choose ten of these positive affirmations and repeat them daily, morning, noon and night, for at least three days at a time. Repeat that process every three days until you have gone through them all. If you really want to supercharge your results, use them <u>all</u> daily for a few weeks (it takes 21 days to form a new habit) and watch how positive your life turns in short order.

Here are your positive affirmations:

"I now choose to release my entire past. It is complete and I AM NOW FREE!"

"I now choose to dissolve all negative self-limiting beliefs. They have NO further power over me."

"I now let go of any and all remaining guilt, distrust, fears, shame, disappointments, resentments, anger, stress, judgements and grudges. I am FREE and CLEAR!"

"All my negative self-images and attitudes are now dissolved."

"I choose to recognize that I am love."

"I choose to realize that I am loved."

"I now realize that I am lovable."

"I choose to see that I am important."

"I am peace."

"I choose to feel joy in my life."

"I choose to be willing to release all resistance to change."

"I choose to deeply and completely love, honor, accept and forgive myself."

"I choose to see that I am the master of my thoughts."

"I choose to see that I am the master of my life."

"I recognize that I am creating the life I want."

"I choose to see that I now know what I want in my life."

"I choose Personal Peace instead of ....(or what I had)."

"I choose to allow my body to effortlessly and easily heal, fully and completely."

"I choose to be happy and healthy."

"It recognize that it is safe for me to speak my truth."

"I choose to be innocent."

"I am innocence itself."

"I choose to be connected to God."

"I choose to remember I have always been connected to God."

"I choose to remember that I could never leave the Presence of God."

"I am fully connected to my Divine source."

"I choose to be trusting, all is unfolding perfectly in my life."

"I choose to recognize that nothing is wrong in my world any longer and everything is fine."

"I choose to see that everything in my world is in perfect order and nothing is out of place."

"I choose to see that nothing needs to be done to make my world better. It is all perfect."

"I choose to trust my own intuition."

"I am Divine unconditional love flowing through every part of my being."

"I choose to be forgiveness in action now."

"I choose to forgive easily and effortlessly everything in my the past and set myself free."

"I see myself as safe and protected no matter where I am."

"I choose to be creative."

"I am a creator."

"I choose that God will create through me."

"I choose to be willing to open my heart to my Self."

"I choose to be patient."

"I am patient."

"I am in perfect alignment with God's plan for me."

"I choose to be more compassionate with others."

"I am compassionate."

"I am compassion itself."

"I am so grateful for all the blessings in my life."

"I choose to take my power back with LOVE."

"I am a radiant expression of GOD."

"I accept myself completely here and now."

"I am a radiant being overflowing with light, love and joy."

"I choose to allow the Light within me to create miracles in my body, mind and affairs."

"I choose to accept my life and everyone in it with more gratitude."

"I choose to express more compassion in my life for everyone."

"I am lovable, even when I don't fully feel it."

"I am learning to love myself."

"I am only a thought away from creating the life I want."

"I am love."

"I am love itself."

"I accept all the blessings life has to offer me."

"I am worthy."

"I am worthy to receive abundance."

"I am ready to receive all kinds of abundance without judgment."

"I love and trust myself completely."

"I allow myself to be myself."

"I am protected at all times."

"I am lovable at all times."

"I choose my thoughts wisely."

"I have unlimited inner resources."

"I delete all remaining negative thoughts or programs."

"I release all remaining negativity."

"I choose kindness."

"I choose compassion."

"I am kindness and compassion personified."

"I forgive myself for not previously changing."

"I forgive myself for retaining the limiting beliefs I still hold."

"I choose a life filled with joy."

"I choose joy over worry."

"I choose love over fear.

"I choose to give rather than receive."

"I am what I think about."

"I become what I think about all day."

"There are no boundaries or limitations to my abundance."

"I have no limit to what I can do.

"There are no limits for me."

"I am learning to love myself."

"I am Present."

"I allow myself to be Present."

"I am Presence first."

"I am a small part of God."

"God is all of me."

"Every part of me is okay."

"I am okay."

"Every part of me works together with every other part."

"Every part of me respects all parts of me."

"All parts of me works well together in cooperation."

"I begin each day with an open heart and mind."

"I choose to begin my day without unnecessary thoughts about yesterday or tomorrow."

"I let go of the past and embrace the Present."

"I relinquish control and listen to the voice of truth within."

"I relinquish mental control and allow God."

"Nothing needs to be done or undone. All is in perfect order all the time."

"Everyone knows everything all the time ... when they allow it."

"I am only a thought away from peace."

"I am only a thought away from inner peace."

"Peace is silence in the face of Truth."

"I am willing to be peaceful now."

"I am able to be peaceful."

"I embrace my own inner peace and stillness."

"I focus on my strength instead of my weakness."

"I put my attention on my strengths and purpose."

"I create peace in my life."

"I embrace the stillness within."

"Everything is perfect in this moment."

"There is no life except in the Present Moment."

"I allow the light within me to shine brightly today."

"I respect myself."

"I no longer allow my past to dictate my future."

"I live fully in the Present Moment."

"I release all negative labels for myself."

"I embrace exactly who I am."

"I am safe at all times."

"I feel protected at all times."

"I am safe and protected at all times."

"I am never truly alone."

"I realize that God/Spirit is always with me."

"I am powerful."

"I am more powerful than I've ever realized before."

"I embrace my inner power and resources."

"I am no longer a victim."

"I never was a victim ... except in my own mind."

"I am always connected to the All."

"I am always in touch with God."

"The Universe is always hugging me."

"I help plant seeds of prosperity and abundance."

"I accept who I am, what I am, and how I am - just as I am."

"I am considerate to myself and all those around me."

"I consider everyone's needs and honor them."

"I honor my own needs at all times."

"I honor myself and all those with whom I come into contact."

"I recognize the value in everything, including myself."

"I respect myself and all those I come in contact with."

"I am strong and healthy."

"My body automatically and naturally heals."

"I send love to every part of my body."

"Every cell in my body responds to the love that I send it."

"Each cell in my body is the embodiment of Love."

"I trust my body."

"I trust my body to heal itself."

"I trust my mind to relinquish control to my Self."

"With each breath I take in, I embrace love and release any thought that doesn't serve me."

"Each breath take brings in healing oxygen to every cell in my body."

"I am whole and complete."

"I am already whole, complete and perfect."

We believe these positive affirmations will fill any voids left from all the work done with EFT, but we also feel that by eliminating your negative thoughts and self-limiting beliefs, you regain your natural happy, peaceful self again without anything extra needing to be added. Of course, we trust these positive affirmations will not only fill any voids, but enhance your life in many ways you never before expected.

Conclusion

You now have a full explanation of EFT, Rapid Reduction of Stress and the Personal Peace Procedure. To get the most benefit from this book, address every specific issue completely and use EFT on it persistently until it is gone. By that, we mean keep doing EFT until you've completely eliminated all of the negatives feelings, stress or self-limiting beliefs. Then, continue doing all of the positive affirmations until you've done them to the point that you're actually feeling positive about yourself, your situation and your feelings. When you do that, you'll find yourself feeling much more peaceful, serene, positive, energetic and happy. In fact, you can expect your life to improve dramatically.

We know this technique will be a big benefit for you if you follow the directions and work at it consistently. Remember, try it on everything and you'll be amazed at the outcome. Good luck!

Peace be with you,
Ted Robinson

NOTIFICATION AND WAIVER

The information contained in this book is presented for informational purposes only. The material is in no way intended to replace professional medical or psychological care or attention by a qualified and licensed practitioner. While we believe that EFT works well with most symptoms, it is still theoretical and there is no universally accepted scientific explanation for its efficacy yet.

Ted Robinson is certified Hypnotists by the National Guild of Hypnotists and other organizations. He is also an Interfaith Minister. While he practices and teaches EFT, he is not a credentialed or licenced therapist or mental health care professional in any area. It should be noted that there are only limited credentials available in EFT so far as it is still in the developmental stages.

Ted believes that all healing has a spiritual basis and that ultimately everyone heals themselves. He does not offer any medical or psychological care or advice other than to advise all clients that each client always remains responsible for their own health care and if they want or need medical, psychological or psychiatric care or advice, they should see a licensed medical or mental health care professional.

Ted advises every client to obtain a waiver or referral from their primary care doctor or other medical professional or their mental health care professional before utilizing EFT on their own or with a practitioner. No client should discontinue or modify any medication presently being taken pursuant to medical advice without obtaining prior medical approval. In the event that a client fails to obtain a medical referral prior to treatment, they assume all risk and sole responsibility for any adverse outcome that might result from using EFT.

The Center for Inner Healing and Ted Robinson assume no liability for any client or third party for any damages or injury which may result from any treatment that has been rendered in good faith in any discipline Please abide by any restrictions placed upon you by your own state laws.

The additional finger points on the diagram page refer to more advanced care using EFT.

All material described herein is either copyrighted or trademarked and may not be used, copied, incorporated or disseminated by any third party without the express prior written approval of the author.

"Hypnosis is the most effective way of giving up smoking, according to the largest scientific comparison."

- New Scientist Magazine

HYPNO-STOPPING
Stop Smoking with Hypnosis

Hypnosis is the best way to stop smoking. By adding EFT to the hypnosis process, you can also eliminate those old emotional urges that tempt you to smoke again.

Hypnosis and Emotional Freedom Technique, when used together, are the most powerful combination in use today to help you become a non-smoker for life.

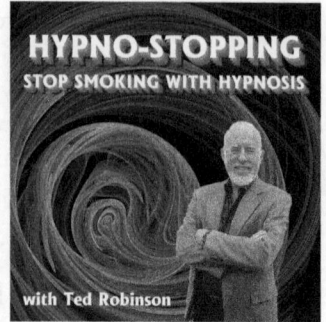

STOP DAILY SMOKING HABITS WITH EMOTIONAL FREEDOM TECHNIQUE

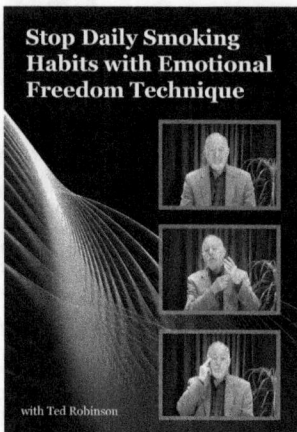

By adding Emotional Freedom Technique to the process, we can eliminate the potential for those old urges coming back and tempting you to smoke again. The two techniques, hypnosis and Emotional Freedom Technique, are absolutely the most effective means of ending your lifetime smoking habit and making you into a non-smoker for life.

Use this video to eliminate any and all habitual urges to smoke throughout the day that may hit you. We all know that we form habits like smoking while reading the paper, during the drive to work, at your coffee break and so on. This video will help you break those habits and once broken, they will not return. The videos are arranged to help you with your urges from the moment you get out of bed all the way to getting up in the middle of the night for that one last cigarette and everything in between. Let us help you become a non-smoker - FOR LIFE!

STOP EMOTIONAL URGES TO SMOKE WITH EFT

By adding Emotional Freedom Technique to the hypnosis process, you eliminate the potential for those old emotional urges to tempt you to smoke again. Hypnosis and Emotional Freedom Technique, when used together, will help you remain a non-smoker for life.

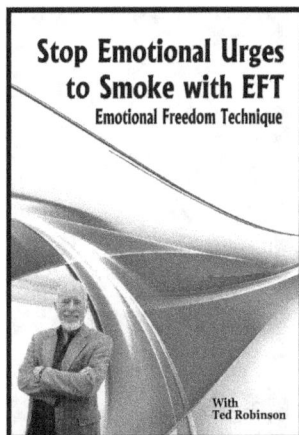

Stop Emotional Urges to Smoke with EFT
Emotional Freedom Technique

With
Ted Robinson

We know that in many situations, emotions arise that can trigger your urge to smoke. You can use this DVD to eliminate those emotional urges to smoke once and for all. The videos are arranged by specific emotions. Use the chapter menu to go directly to the video that addresses your emotional issue and tap along with it. It will help you remain a non-smoker - FOR LIFE!

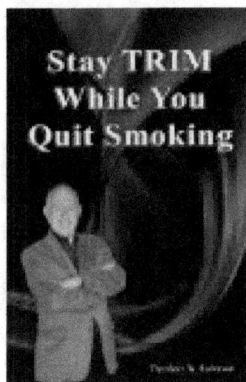

Stay TRIM While You Quit Smoking

STAY TRIM WHILE YOU QUIT SMOKING
Written Specifically for Men

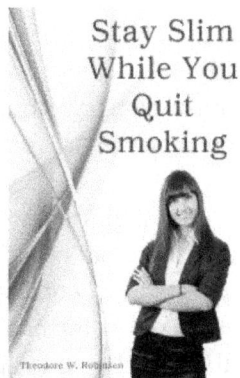

Stay Slim While You Quit Smoking

STAY SLIM WHILE YOU QUIT SMOKING
Written Specifically for Women

Many people refuse to quit smoking because they are afraid they will gain weight. As a result, they remain smokers and keep killing themselves one cigarette at a time. These books will support you while you quit smoking and help you stay slim and trim as you quit. This book will teach you Emotional Freedom Technique, the most powerful way to eliminate the underlying emotional triggers to over-eating as you quit smoking. It's almost like magic when you use it. Also included in the book are easy to prepare, low calorie meals, dessert and snack recipes to give you enjoyable food ideas and help you to stay slim and trim at the same time.

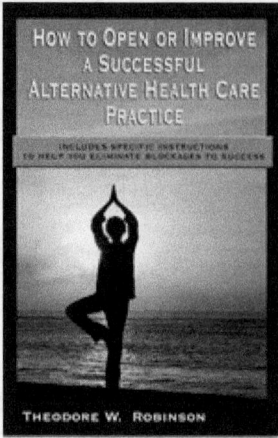

HOW TO OPEN AND IMPROVE A SUCCESSFUL ALTERNATIVE HEALTH CARE PRACTICE

This book will help you become the professional you can be in the burgeoning field of alternative health care. It contains marketing information, credit repair advice and a host of other things you will need to open your own practice or to improve an existing practice.

108 WAYS TO MARKET YOUR PRACTICE

This book is a practical guide for success for holistic and alternative health care practitioners. It has a heavy emphasis on web related marketing techniques and unique ideas on how to jump start a new practice. There many additional topics including Unique Selling Propositions, how to overcome procrastination and eliminating resistance to change.

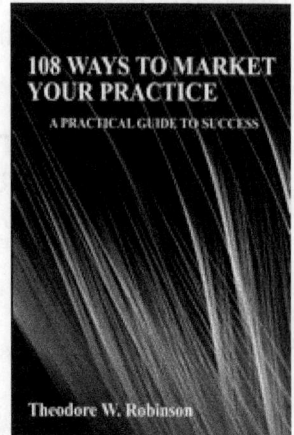

There is an entire appendix which teaches how to do Emotional Freedom Technique (EFT) and gives specific wording to achieve business success. This book will help everyone from the beginner to the seasoned practitioner with new ideas, new methods and unique approaches to achieve success.

If you want to learn more about our products,
visit our website at www.innerhealingpress.com.

You may contact Ted Robinson by phone at (516) 248-5346
or by email at ted@tedrobinson.com

www.ingramcontent.com/pod-product-compliance
Lightning Source LLC
LaVergne TN
LVHW051702080426
835511LV00017B/2676